CW01186916

laneman publishing

Carp Tales 2

EDITED BY PAUL SELMAN

ILLUSTRATED BY PETE CURTIS

A collection of humorous fishing stories by

Jim Gibbinson
Des Taylor
Brian Skoyles
Julian Cundiff
Tony Miles
Tim Paisley
Peter Sharpe
Derek Stritton
Chris Woodrow
Bob Roberts
Axeman
Dave Lane
Chris Ball
Paul Selman
Chris Tarrant

Carp Tales 2 - a limited edition book.
Published in November 2001 by
Laneman Publishing, 5 Lyons Court,
Dorking, Surrey RH4 1AB
© Laneman Publishing 2001

All rights reserved. No part of this publication may be reproduced or transmitted in any form or by any means, electronic or mechanical, including photocopy, recording, or any information storage and retrieval system without permission in writing from the publishers.

British Library Cataloguing in Publication Data
A catalogue record for this book is available from the British Library.
ISBN 1-901717-09-7
Production by Lane Design. Telephone: 01306 875154
Printed in Great Britain.

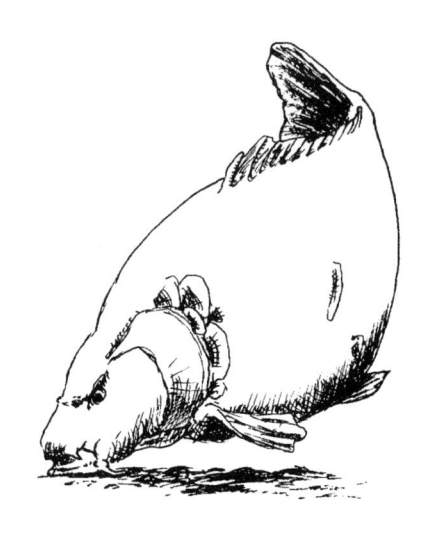

Price £14.95

Carp Reflections (2nd edition)
by Paul Selman

An Obsession with Carp
by Dave Lane

the Myth
by Keith Jenkins

Carp Tales
edited by Paul Selman

Gravel Pit Carp
by Jim Gibbinson

Catch Carp
with Andy Murray

Chasing Dreams
by Tony Miles

Fish the Midlands
with Des Taylor

For full details telephone
01925 768948
or e.mail sales@laneman.co.uk
or on the Internet at www.laneman.co.uk

Introduction

After the success of Carp Tales 1 in 1998, many readers asked for a follow-up book. So Carp Tales 2 was inevitable really, and I think many will find this volume even better than Carp Tales 1.

Other than Dave Lane's brilliant chapter - a genuine classic - which I make no apologies for reproducing from his best-selling book, An Obsession With Carp, all the remaining chapters have been especially commissioned, and have never before been published. I am really delighted and proud that Chris Tarrant took the time out of his busy TV schedule to write his wonderful contribution to the book. I know he was a tad surprised at being asked to contribute, but he was also very pleased. His chapter brings back many fond memories for me of the carp fishing of the 1970's, and of the larger-than-life Duncan Kay! I must commit my own favourite 'Duncan' stories to print one day!

I am also very pleased to launch two brand new talented writers onto the carp scene, in the form of Peter Sharpe and Rob 'The Axeman' Fryer. These two have been gathering quite a following since they began writing on the www.fishingwarehouse.co.uk website I front up, and when you read their sparkling chapters you'll understand why.

This is a wonderful book. Enjoy it.

Paul Selman
Cheshire, November 2001

Acknowledgements

I'd like to thank the following for all playing their part in Carp Tales 2.

Thanks to all the contributors for their brilliant chapters. Chris Tarrant, Chris Ball, Jim Gibbinson, Bob Roberts, Tim Paisley, Derek Stritton, Brian Skoyles, Julian Cundiff, Rob Fryer, Peter Sharpe, Chris Woodrow, Dave Lane, Tony Miles and Des Taylor. Thanks for your personal support and huge encouragement.

All the characters in my chapter, for enriching my life and making me smile. Wherever you are dear Jon, save a swim for me.

My friend, Pete Curtis, for the wonderful illustrations as always.

Stephen Lane, for making it all come together.

To Wendy, for the additional proofing and keeping me relatively sane.

Carp Tales 2

Carp Tales 2

Contents

Introduction 3

Chapter 1 **Jim Gibbinson** 6
 No adulation for eavesdroppers

Chapter 2 **Des Taylor** 17
 "When men were men and women were glad of them"

Chapter 3 **Brian Skoyles** 24
 Ducks, animals and a steaming crotch

Chapter 4 **Julian Cundiff** 37
 I wish I didn't have to remember!

Chapter 5 **Tony Miles** 47
 Carp tales comedy

Chapter 6 **Tim Paisley** 57
 You didn't mean to do that, did you?

Chapter 7 **Derek Stritton** 68
 French connection

Chapter 8 **Peter Sharpe** 76
 Night fever

Chapter 9 **Chris Woodrow** 83
 Essex man

Chapter 10 **Bob Roberts** 92
 Uninvited guests

Chapter 11 **Rob 'Axeman' Fryer** 102
 Adolf and the Shoulder Monster

Chapter 12 **Dave Lane** 120
 Battle of the pikeys

Chapter 13 **Chris Ball** 125
 Photographic faux pas and camouflage

Chapter 14 **Paul Selman** 137
 All creatures great and small

Chapter 15 **Chris Tarrant** 151
 The glorious 16th!

No adulation for eavesdroppers

by Jim Gibbinson

"Well, I'm surprised to see you here!"

The words were spoken by someone I didn't recognise, but who obviously recognised me. The 'here' in question being a small gravel-pit-cum-farm-reservoir. My visitor then explained that he assumed I spent my time on exclusive, heavily stocked big-fish waters, not on small pits - however pretty they might be - that could be fished by anyone who bought a club card.

It would appear that such a view is fairly typical. Additionally, it is widely believed that 'known' anglers, especially if they are writers as well, spend their fishing lives in some sort of angling Nirvana - a blissful existence where the best swims are never taken, the weather is always perfect and the fish can be guaranteed to feed. Furthermore, it is presumed that their trips are exemplar models of efficiency where nothing ever goes wrong.

Then there's the esteem in which celebrity anglers are held, and the respect they are accorded - after all, famous people in other walks of life are deified by an adoring public, so surely the same thing happens with angling writers?

You reckon?

While it is true that there are hero-worshippers who have an unrealistic perception of well-known anglers' abilities, there are also those who harbour simmering resentment and pass up no opportunity to make disparaging comments. Take the incident which occurred at RMC's Sutton at Hone water. An angler in the next swim came along to watch me play a fish - he'd evidently heard my Delkim and thought I'd hooked a carp. It was a bream as it turned out, but he stayed for a chat anyway.

After a few minutes he returned to his pitch. I re-baited and recast. A short time later I heard a loud, raucous voice; it belonged to a new arrival who had stopped behind my neighbour. He didn't know I was there because I was tucked below the top of the bank, semi-hidden from view.

"I hear Gibbo's fishing here," he said; then after the briefest of pauses added, "sad b*****d!"

Jim waiting for a fish and having a chat, without any hassle this time!

This condemnatory comment was followed by urgent mutterings, which I presume were warnings from my neighbour that I was close by! There was then a short silence, during which time my censorious critic was doubtless considering his position. He decided that rather than be compelled to pass me, he would stomp off in the opposite direction; but as he did so - and this is the bit I really liked - he called back over his shoulder,

"I still think he's a sad b*****d."

Not one of my more ardent fans, then!

Mugged

Insults I can take; bankside robbery is another matter entirely.

It happened while I was fishing Johnson's Road Lake from a swim known as 'The Beach'. It was one of my favourite swims on the pit - something of a sun trap, in fact - and clean underfoot due to its composition of sand, gravel and shingle. A short time previously I'd seen a carp head-and-shoulder about fifteen yards out - not far beyond where my right-hand bait lay. I had seen a couple of tench roll too, so I was confident of action.

Suddenly, from behind a clump of trees, bounded a black, slavering Baskervillian monster that looked like a three-way cross between a Rottweiler, a bull mastiff and a rhino! God, it was ugly! It made straight for my groundbait bowl in which lay a couple of kilos of Method-mix. With a dreadful slurping, growling sound, it thrust its head deep in the bowl and devoured the lot! It then ran off in the direction of its owner. The whole incident had lasted no more than about five seconds.

I had been mugged!

By a dog!

So why didn't I intervene?

Well, partly, as already mentioned, because I was taken unawares by the sheer speed of the incident. By the time I had collected my senses, it was all over. Then there was the creature itself. It was big, I mean really big. It looked aggressive, too. In the normal course of events, I am not scared of dogs - I don't like them, but they don't intimidate me. This beast, however, was in a league of its own.

Then there was its owner.

Imagine, if you will, a tall, thickset figure who stood there in that 'well hard' bowed arms and legs posture adopted by the muscle-bound. I concluded that remonstrating with him would probably result in my getting thumped, so I settled for a look of exasperated displeasure.

As he returned my gaze, his coarse features formed into a scowl. Then, to my relief, he turned away and with a gruff, "Gerrin," he ordered the dog into his Shogun and drove off.

I was seething - not so much at the incident itself, but at the indifference and discourtesy shown by the guy - so I plotted my revenge.

At which juncture, and so as not to build up your hopes of a sensational denouement to the story, I have to tell you that while I devised what I considered to be an appropriate scheme, I never had the opportunity to put my plan into effect. My intended retaliation was so elegant in its conception, however, that I consider it worth recording.

Mixing some groundbait - but no dogs in sight this time!

Its central element was a fast acting, powerful purgative. It would do the dog no harm, but in the short-term was guaranteed to produce dramatic results. I won't disclose what the substance was - suffice it to say that I sought expert advice from a pharmacist friend. My plan was to keep the medicament to hand, and apply it to my Method-mix next time the ghastly creature hove into view. If events proceeded as before, it would wolf down the groundbait, rush back to its owner and climb on the leather-clad back seat of the Shogun. For a short time all would be well, but suddenly and without warning - and almost certainly while they were still in the vehicle - the purgative would take explosive effect..!

Oh, what a wonderful vision that evokes!

To my disappointment, despite fishing the swim on a number of subsequent occasions, neither the cursed cur nor its Neanderthal owner showed up again.

Secret pool

What was I saying earlier about monster-filled, exclusive waters?

Nowadays there are plenty of such places, but if we go back to a time before the importation - legal and otherwise - of huge continental specimens, there were very few waters which held exceptionally large fish. But we could dream - and most of us harboured a faint hope that we would one day find our own version of Redmire. During the close-season we studied Ordnance Survey maps and visited every patch of blue within reasonable travelling distance. Rumours, no matter how vague and unpromising, were followed up, too.

Which situation led to the incident I am about to describe.

My friend Len Burgess and I were fishing adjacent swims in a small, local gravel pit when a young angler - late teens, I would guess - stopped to speak with us,

"You after carp?"

We confirmed that we were.

"I caught a seventeen pounder last weekend."

I looked up, "Nice; where from?"

"Vixen's Pool."

"Where's that?"

"Near Maidstone."

Len and I knew the area very well, and we thought we'd explored every water shown on the map, even the one which an erstwhile luminary had stocked with carp 'donated' (albeit unwittingly!) by a local club - but that, as they say, is another story! We had not, however, come across Vixen's Pool, so we obtained detailed directions from our young visitor, along with the information,

"You get tickets from a lady who lives in a cottage next to the lake."

We were also assured that there were carp in the lake much bigger than his seventeen pounder.

"How much bigger?" we asked.

He held out his arms at full stretch - which we did not take literally, of course, but concluded that even when ratcheted down a few notches, these could be seriously big fish.

After the youngster had gone, Len turned to me with a smile and said,

"This might be it - our own personal Redmire."

I was always less of a dreamer than Len, but I conceded that Vixen's Pool had to be worth investigating.

The following weekend we set off for a reconnoitre. On arrival at the farm track described by our young informant, we parked the car and walked towards the cottage. There, set in a slight hollow, lay a pond. We had been warned that it was, quote, 'not very big', but we were entirely unprepared for what confronted us. In trying to convey to you just how small it was, the word 'tiny' springs to mind, but on reflection I think 'microscopic' is better! The real Redmire would have been positively oceanic by comparison - even Patshull Bridge Pool (which I calculate to be one nineteenth of an acre), would seem huge. Have you seen Constable's painting, 'The Haywain' (otherwise known as 'Prat in a Pond')? Well, you could have dropped Vixen's Pool in it several times - and that without removing the haywain! No one was fishing, but had a couple of anglers been seated opposite one another, and had they been using float-rods, they would have needed to take care that their tips did not clash! We are - as you will have gathered - talking minuscule!

If the water itself was diminutive, the amount of fishable bank space was practically sub-molecular. This was on account of a fence, which came down to the water's edge halfway along one bank, and continued on the opposite bank. Its purpose being to separate the bank which could be fished from that which constituted the owner's garden. Also, presumably, it served to prevent the resident free-range chickens from ranging too freely!

Len and I looked at each other, shook our heads in disbelief, and turned to walk back to the car. At that moment came a woman's voice,

"Hello - do you want tickets?"

Len pursed his lips in mock concentration,

"No thanks," he said, "you can't fish the best end."

I spluttered as I choked back the laugh that was welling up inside me - after all, I didn't want to offend her. Len merely smiled innocently as he waved the bemused woman a cheery good-bye.

"You can't fish the best end," has since become one of our stock phrases. Size is immaterial; nor does it need to have a fenced-off end to qualify. It just means,

"I don't much fancy this place."

Fishing a slightly larger pool than Vixen's Pool.

Norwich night life
Len figures in this account, too. It occurred when we were on one of our periodic pike trips to the Norfolk Broads - or to be more precise, to Hoveton Great Broad. In those days - and perhaps now, for all I know - Hoveton was strictly private, but I had been fortunate in gaining permission to fish from the estate manager. Whether it was home to bigger pike than other broads, I don't know - but it was a stunningly beautiful place, and there's something special about having a private water all to oneself.

I'd had some good catches from the broad in previous trips, but on this occasion it was not to be - our first day was a complete blank. We had no idea why - the weather was okay, the water looked good, too. Still, no matter, we had a second day available and, being the eternal optimists, we were convinced we'd find some pike (we did, but only one each).

We booked ourselves into a small commercial hotel near Norwich town centre, and after a hasty wash and a change of clothes we went to look for somewhere to eat. Admittedly this was winter, but virtually everywhere was shut - after half an hour of exploration we'd been unable to find either a Chinese or Indian restaurant, or even a pub which offered food. Our options exhausted, we settled for a Kentucky Fried Chicken establishment. This was very much a last resort - and I don't say that to denigrate Colonel Sanders's efforts, but simply because I've never been a big fan of fried food.

The place was devoid of customers; no staff members were anywhere to be seen, either. This, coupled with the fact that several tables were cluttered with used plates and drinks containers, gave the premises a sort of Mary Celeste ambience. But we were hungry, so we took a seat and awaited the arrival of the waitress.

Waiting table can be a dispiriting job - I know because back in my student days I did it - but how much energy does it take to muster up a smile? This small social grace, however, was either too much effort or constituted a skill yet to be mastered by the sullen faced teenager who eventually came to our table. She didn't ask us what we wanted; she just stood there - her cheerless face totally devoid of any expression. In an attempt to lighten the mood and evoke a flicker of amusement, I looked up at her and asked,

"Have you got chicken?"

I hadn't expected her eyes to light up, nor did I think her face would show unbridled joy in response to my attempt at levity, but I thought something would register. But no. Nothing at all.

"What do you want wiv it?"

"What have you got?" I asked.

She hesitated - doubtless waiting for a synapse to make its connection - then replied,

"Chips."

Proving that Len catches pike as well as visiting the hotspots of Norfolk.

"Do you have anything else?"
Another pause. "No."
"Chips then, please."
"Two?"
"I'd rather hoped for about half a plateful."

This, my second attempt at levity, fell on even stonier ground than the first. She looked blank - so blank in fact that I feared she had suffered a neural shutdown. Somewhat alarmed, I smiled in what I hoped was a reassuring manner and said,

"Yes, two please."

Following our meal, we decided to find a pub. Now, I accept that we may have been unlucky, but just as the KFC place was deserted, so was the pub! Well, almost. It's sole occupants - the barman apart - comprised a skinny little guy in his forties, with his hair so slicked down that it looked like PVC, and a grossly overweight woman who sat next to him. They looked like those incongruous couples portrayed on seaside postcards. Len and I, by the act of entering, had doubled the pub's clientele!

As we sat, drinking our beer and discussing prospects for the following day, I noticed from the corner of my eye that PVC-hair had left his seat. I assumed he was going to the bar - but no, he went to a small dais, picked up a microphone, blew into it, tapped it a few times, and proceeded to sing! For whom he was singing, and why, I'm not quite sure. Nor do I know whether he was the official musical entertainment, or merely Norwich's forerunner to karaoke. He sang unaccompanied, and in that peculiar manner which Reeves and Mortimer call 'club style.' The technique is unique to pubs, and is characterised by its distorted vowels and the insertion of lots of inappropriate 'h' sounds.

"H-please, h-release me, set me fr-hee," he sang,
"Hai don't h-love you h-any mo-ooore..."

I was absolutely fascinated, not only by the style of singing, but by the seriousness with which PVC-hair took himself. Indeed, I was so fascinated that our intended pint became two, then three, before I could tear myself away and return to our hotel.

The whole evening, with its deserted premises and bizarre cast list, had a somewhat surreal feel to it - not unlike The League of Gentlemen's fictitious village of Royston Vasey!

The episode occurred about twenty years ago, and no doubt Norwich has since developed into a culinary, cultural and lively metropolis.

But I wouldn't know. I've never been back!

Barefoot in the dark

Having strayed from my 'carp tales' brief by including an account of a pike trip, I'll now stray yet further and describe something which occurred while sea fishing.

Back in my teacher-training days, when I was a student in Durham, I made regular night-time cod fishing trips to the Blast Beach near Dawdon Colliery. I didn't have any means of transport so I was dependent on buses.

To reach the Blast Beach it was necessary to descend a narrow and occasionally precipitous cliff path - a 'hairy' procedure at the best of times, and even more so when it was made slippery by frost or snow. The beach itself comprised shale, and was always littered with driftwood and broken pit-props. Not the most picturesque of spots, but the best cod beach I have ever fished.

On the night in question I arrived on the last bus, descended the frozen cliff path without mishap and found, as was often the case, that the beach was deserted. After collecting wood, and lighting my wigwam shaped fire, I tackled up and started fishing. The wind, which had been brisk since my arrival, gained strength - not too much, but enough to make casting somewhat difficult.

I caught a couple of cod, and was confident of a few more when I noticed that the wind was getting appreciably stronger. Sparks flew horizontally from my fire, spume blew from the wave tops, and froth ran high up the beach. In the darkness beyond, I could hear the crashing of the breakers - but hey, this was the North Sea in the middle of winter for heaven's sake, and a bit of rough weather was to be expected.

Then it happened.

An exceptionally large breaker smashed on the beach and rushed up the shale towards me. It enveloped and extinguished my fire, thereby plunging me in darkness, and rapidly rose to my thighs. For a few seconds I was disorientated, unable to see and surrounded by swirling water as the undertow tried to drag me towards the oncoming breakers. I attempted to scramble higher up the beach but the current shifted the shale beneath my feet, causing me to lose my balance and fall in the water. Briefly I was completely submerged. They say that your life flashes before your eyes on such occasions, but I can't recollect any such thing happening - I suspect panic overwhelmed my brain and blotted out everything other than my immediate predicament. How I managed to resist being dragged out to sea, I'll never know - frankly, I think it was just luck that as the water receded it relinquished its hold.

I lurched unsteadily up the beach - incongruously I still held my rod. Of the rest of my gear, there was no sign.

When I was sufficient distance from the water to be safe, and had recovered my senses somewhat, I considered my options. It was the middle of the night, I was absolutely drenched, and I was marooned on Dawdon's Blast Beach with no immediate means of getting back to Durham. The next bus was six or seven hours away. I knew it would be foolhardy to try to endure a winter's night on an exposed beach in wet clothing - so I decided to walk. The prospect filled me with despair because it was approximately fourteen miles from Dawdon to Durham - but what choice did I have?

After the first couple of miles my wet feet started to blister - so I removed my boots and carried them. In which state - barefoot, bedraggled and soaked to the skin; a rod in one hand and boots under my arm - I trudged the remaining twelve miles along deserted, darkened roads.

As you can imagine, I was immensely relieved when I finally arrived back at the student hostel and dragged my weary, frozen body up the stairs to my room. But after a hot shower and a few hours sleep, I was looking at tide tables and planning my next trip.

Are we all daft, or is it just me?

Jim relaxing.

"When men were men and women were glad of them"

by Des Taylor

I suppose in every angler's life there is a period that you remember with extra fondness and wish those days could have gone on forever....

Such a period for me was around the mid-seventies when it was still "old England."

Men went down the pub, women were there to have children and keep house and above all we were fishing for just fun and nothing else.

Admittedly the "twenty" or bust mentality was starting to creep in, but only just.

This was still a time when if you caught one twenty in a summer with a few doubles you were doing well. In fact, as a Midlander if you caught two twenties in a summer you were a liar! These were the dark days before Matt Hayes and Total Fishing.

Des Taylor.

This was a period when Terry Eustace sat in his house in the dark practising tying knots without any light. A period when I was not allowed in the British Carp Study Group because I knew Ron Felton, and a period when Chris Yates caught his first twenty-pound carp on a white moth. Yes, even then, Chris was working at a slight tangent to the rest of us!

Chris caught that twenty from a lake in mid-Wales in the heart of the town of Llandrindod Wells. In the seventies this was the place to be, as many a budding famous angler had his first taste of carp fishing at this angling Mecca. Anglers like John Lilley, Ron Felton, Billy Walkeden, John Freeman, Dave Parkes and Phil Pearson were all weaned on this shallow water in sleepy mid-Wales.

But let's not talk about the size of the fish, these were the days when young men had character. In fact, these same men have come through to the modern day and are the only characters left in the angling world. How sad!

These characters left etched in my mind the things that went on in those days, some that cannot even be reproduced for this book and best took to the grave. However, here is a selection of stories of the crazy days spent on that water in the '70's. The names might not be exactly correct - in fact some of these stories may be prone to slight exaggeration with the passing of time, but basically the story line is correct and I hope you enjoy your time at Llandrindod Wells.

So, let's go back to the time when men were men and women were glad of them....

My first story relates to a young man from South Wales who took life at times a little too seriously. You see in time gone by we believed carp would eat par boiled potatoes. In fact, only one carp in any lake once a year would eat one but we all continued to use them. I cannot ever remember having a run on a potato, but I always had one on one of the rods. There you go. I blame it on the drugs, beer and music of that period... However, this guy had great faith in potatoes and the ones the size of a Jersey Mid with a size 2 VMC stuck into it.

He would put crust on the top of it and bottom of it, so the hook would never pull out even when he struck - so he never had much chance like the rest of us of hooking a fish on this bait. We didn't care - for catching carp was not the objective. To be carp fishing was good enough. Indeed some anglers didn't even want a run - they bathed in the glory of rod hours without a carp.

Back to the guy from South Wales.....

I don't know if you have found the same - but there are two kinds of Welshmen.

The first and thankfully the biggest majority are great people who enjoy life and don't give a toss. Then there's the other Welsh people who are the tightest, most boring, biggest whingers in the world. You know the type?

This guy was one from the second category and had gone weeks fishing small par-boiled spuds on both rods without even a single bleep. Every morning he woke from a fish-less night he would shout along the lake in his very dull Welsh accent,

"I reckon this lake is biologically bolloxed, that's four weekends without a run. I reckon all the carp are bloody dead in this cess-pit."

This went on for most of that summer and to be honest, his views were starting to dampen the rest of the anglers' enthusiasm on the lake. However typical of this lovely period - there was always a practical joke around the corner to lighten the mood. One night the lads waited for the Welshman to cast his potatoes out and fall fast asleep. The buzzers in those days were the Heron design, which were based on the antennae principle, which to be honest were crap compared to the designs of modern day buzzers.

Nevertheless it put excitement into your fishing in that you always worried whether they would work or not on your next run.... but I digress....

The lads took the Welshman's line from around the antennae and reeled both rods in. Then they removed the small par-boiled potatoes and replaced them with two huge - and I mean huge - peeled King Edward potatoes.

Such was the weight of these things they couldn't be cast out they had to be thrown out by hand.

Through all this the Welshman slept soundly.

In the morning as usual - having had another blank night - when he reeled in he felt a weight. Could it be a fish?

The Welshman shouted loudly,

"I think a crucian or a small mirror has hooked itself," as he reeled in the weight.

Then imagine his face when the huge potato hit the surface.

The Welshman stood there for a while in sheer shock with the King Edward in his hand.

The rest of us were hiding our faces behind sleeping bag, trees and cars.

Suddenly, the Welshman uttered the most profound statement I have ever heard in carp angling history.

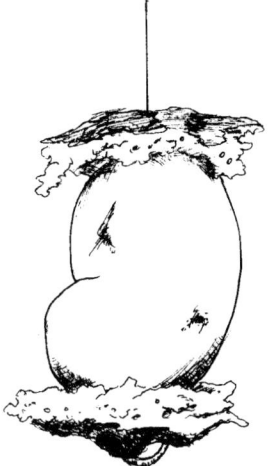

"I told you this water was biologically bolloxed - look at what it has done to my spuds in 12 hours of being in the water!"

As if that wasn't funny enough, try to imagine the Welshman's face when he reeled in his second rod and the same happened again. It was quite a while before we saw that lad again. In fact, I think he now resides in a monastery near Abergavenny - such was the shock!

The next couple of stories relate to an Irish angler called Jim Burke. Now Jim was an eel, pike and carp man. He talked with a Brummie accent but was originally from across the Irish Sea and was and still is one of the dying breed of great characters. Jim is a lovely bloke but in those days could be, well, physical for the sake of a better phrase.

Llandrindod Wells was an inland holiday resort and not only carp anglers were around the lake. There were young ladies willing to bend over backwards to help anyone - if you get my drift. There were also moms and dads with children and even young men and women left over from the forgotten world of the hippies. One such man with hair down to his shoulders, a goatee beard and clothes that had obviously been brought from the Oxfam shop in the centre of the town, was a frequent visitor.

Jim was lying on his garage bought-bedchair fishing the dam end of the lake when this hippie walked past. "Hi man. Make love not war, peace man," said the hippie to Jim.

Now I didn't think for one minute Jim believed what this guy was saying and returned with words something along the lines of,

"Do you mean to say you don't believe in violence at all and you only believe in love not war?"

The hippie replied, "Yes man. You can throw me in the lake and I would forgive you man."

Jim couldn't believe his luck and never one to miss a chance of a giggle, promptly got off his chair.

"You know, I've been looking for a guy like you all my life," said Jim.

The hippie looked confused, but soon wised up as Jim proceeded to grab his collar and the arse of his pants and slung him out into the depths of the lake.

Rumour has it that later the hippy

became a Chelsea skinhead and never said daft things like that again - at least not with water nearby!

Another very short story about Jim Burke. There was a famous angler who fished Llandrindod Wells who only caught carp there when no one was around. You only needed to slip to the café for a packet of smokes and he would catch a couple of doubles and he also had the knack of hooking, landing and returning 20's - without the two swims either side of him hearing a thing.

That's a skill that has been operated by a number of famous anglers in the past... but let's move on.

Jim Burke said of this angler that even if he saw the guy strike the rod, Jim land the fish for him and then take the photographs himself of the guy he would not believe the capture - till he had the photographs back!

Rumour has it that Jim and his mates put cigarette ends on the spreader block of the man's landing net before darkness on an all-night session. Next morning the famous liar in question always reckoned that he had caught three doubles and a twenty. However when the lads checked the butt-ends of the cigarettes they had not moved an inch!

Now that's skill and proves that even in days gone by there was an unknown skill to being a famous angler!

One last story from Llandrinrod Wells. It relates to a Midlands angler who wanted to be as good as the "southern twitcher-hitters."

We in the Midlands were in awe of the likes of Jim Gibbinson, with the fast-taper Clooper rods, high rod rests and painted needles and their ability to hook carp that only moved the line a few inches.

We were still waiting for the silver paper or my bread dough to get stuck in the butt ring!

That was until one night when my bread dough was so big to counteract the tow that it got stuck in the butt ring and a carp took my rod and reel to the island before I could wake up!

However, those southerners had moved on and they were wearing combat jackets while we still wore donkey jackets with leather patches on the shoulders. They were using secret pastes from the world of birdseed and one guy named Bob Morris had caught a hundred doubles in a season when in the Midlands we didn't have a hundred doubles to catch!

Most of us just read about these southern experts. However, this one guy had jumped in his car and went and fished down there with them. It's hard to believe now with anglers travelling all over the world to catch carp - but in the seventies if you couldn't get there by using two buses - it was on another planet. In fact, travelling from Birmingham to Llandrindod was classed as the premier division of carp angling travellers! For weeks the guy spent time talking, listening and fishing with these southerners.

When he returned to Llandrindod he had changed to a southerner. He had become conceited, big headed, had a big engine in his car and even said things like, "Want to buy a watch, my old son?"

Before he had gone down south he hardly said a thing - now he knew everything and you couldn't get a word in edgeways!

Boy, had he got some north and south... spoke a lot of times on the ham bone... had a lot of bother with his trouble and strife and in general got on everyone's tits!

Pay-back time was only just around the corner!

He would stand next to his rods for hours on end and with the majestic strike of a bronzed warrior he would hit a twitch and another carp was landed.

The rest of us struggled to catch fish but this lad with his southern ways was emptying the place.

Jealously did not come into it. No, forget what I have just said. Jealously was the only motive when we got our own back!

On the night in question, the adopted southerner was set up on a swim known as The Oaks. In this swim you could sleep in your car on the road right next to the rods, so obviously it was a popular swim with the long-session boys. He had cast his fast tapered rods further than we could walk and had already had two or three twitches to the net.

The rest of us were still praying for a run on potatoes - with no luck at all.

Now a thing a lot of people didn't know about Llandrindod was that it was full of crucian carp, and every September and October just before the start of the pike season some of us would put our 42" landing nets into the margins baited with bread.

After an hour or so, we would net out half a dozen small crucians to take home with us. Illegal transferring of fish was something we knew nothing of in those days. Indeed most of the carp from Llandrindod Wells ended up in Midlands' lakes - but that is best left well alone. Anyway, we used this ploy one evening to get six crucians and kept them in the keep net for later to utilise Plan A.

The plan worked a treat. What it entailed was that we waited for the said angler to fall asleep in his Ford Anglia with the done up engine.

Then we reeled in one of his rods, took off the paste bait and threaded six crucians on his big hook. These we cast out into the lake and then put the rod back onto the buzzer and awaited the fun.

"Bleep, bleep...." went the buzzers, with no response from the Ford Anglia.

"Bleep, bleep...." again went the buzzers.

In fact they sounded for around thirty minutes before the lazy git got out of the car!

When he did, all hell broke loose for he tripped over - knocking gear all over the place. Eventually he managed to strike and with it came the usual, "I'm in again, my son!"

This was in a London accent - even though he came from near Stoke!

Of course the six crucians each pulled in different ways and fought like only six crucians on one hook really could!

The boy was confused to say the least!

As he reeled in, the fish came to the surface and in the dark the angler was lost for words... Suddenly he cried, "I think I've hooked a baby catfish or something strange."

With that most of us at the lake nearly fell in the water with laughter ...but then came the punch-line. After winding the fish up the dam and into his hands he realised what he had got.

Now a real Midlander would have surely realised he had just had the urinal taken out of him. However this guy had got it bad and thought himself so good.

He shouted out aloud in the darkness of that Welsh valley lake, "Look what I've done. Am I not the greatest twitcher-hitter of all time? I've hooked a shoal of feeding crucians - in one strike!" And he bloody believed it!

Rumour has it that like a lot of anglers that fished that place around that time, he is now residing in a special home in the country - which is so posh it has padded walls.

As I said. This was a time when men were men and women were glad of them. God knows why!

Ducks, animals and a steaming crotch

by Brian Skoyles

Anyone who had been fishing seriously for over forty years will have a tale or two to tell, and I'm no exception. Probably the most memorable session I've ever had, has already featured in Carp Tales 1. It was called The Session from Hell and was rightly written up by Bill Cottam. Over the years I've had some great sessions with Bill, and it's his crotch that gets a mention in this effort, but more of that later.

I hope you get as much pleasure from what follows, as I've had thinking back to compile my collection of personal memorabilia.

One of the nice things about carp fishing is that it often gives you, not only moments to remember, but also the time to remember them. How often have you sat outside a bivvy with a mate or two, brew in hand, and the conversation starts, "Do you remember the session when ....?"

When I look back, at my collection of "Do you remember when's ...," most of them seem to feature livestock of one kind or another ...and I'm not talking about Bill's crotch again!

Take the ducks who didn't like water for example ....

I seem to have this affinity for water, in that it often seems that when I go fishing it pees it down. One particular session on Waveney Valley E Lake was no exception.

Now this was the early eighties, and there weren't many different bivvies to choose from, and the days of one man this, two man that, Titans, Big Boys etc. were yet to come. I was the proud owner of a Dave Barnes Aqua-Shelter. At the time these were state of the art shelters. Basically they fitted over a standard brollie, then had parallel sides that you staked to the ground. Then you tied garden canes to each corner to stop the sides flapping. The bedchair then fitted in behind the middle pole (In theory you could remove this centre brollie pole, and the brollie would rest on the garden canes... mine used to collapse sideways instead). The entrance was very much like today's over-wrap systems in that you could zip up two zips to roll up one side panel.

At the time these were very well made, quality shelters, and I spent many a night in mine, before it eventually gave up the ghost.

Back to Waveney Valley. I was set up on the first main peg on E Lake fishing along the side of the spit, and into the corner. The rain was seriously hard, and to make it even more uncomfortable was being blown directly into my bivvy door by a fairly strong wind. I was two days into the session, and hadn't had a blip. I didn't see any reason why the second night should be any different, so opted to settle into the sleeping bag fairly early. I also opted to try and keep some of the rain out as well, and zipped the door down to within a foot of the ground, but tied the bottom bit of the door upwards, so I had this gap that I could see out of when I was laid down.

Brian's early bivvy.

In those days you didn't have remote buzzer extensions, and in heavy rain you couldn't always count on the buzzer anyhow, so it was usual practice to make sure you could see your rods.

I gradually got warm, and lay there listening to the rain battering the bivvy. Through the narrow gap I could see the rods and the stationary bobbins, and the occasional disgruntled duck walking past the entrance.

I must have drifted off to sleep.

Beeeeeep .....Beeeeeep .... Beeeeeeeeeeeeeeeee ....

My buzzer! A run, I shot up, and all hell broke loose!

It's pitch black. I'm half in, half out of a sleeping bag with a mind of its own. I'm in a shelter with the door zipped down to within in a foot of the ground, and at least six startled ducks try to take off.

I suppose I was quiet and still, and these ducks had fancied a bit of time out of the rain. The gap I'd left was nice and handy to waddle through and they had settled down for a bit of a kip. Me shooting bolt upright, had panicked them a little, and they'd not found the entrance as easily, on the way out.

It was mayhem! A total shamble of feathers, flapping wings, scrabbling feet, fishing gear, and at least one incontinent mallard.

Eventually I found the zip, opened the door, and crawled out.

The run? ....I missed that!

I suppose you could say, I was out for a duck!

Then there was the night stalking session at Emmotland...

One of the happiest periods of my angling life, was the time spent at Emmotland. For two or three years I must have been one of the luckiest carp anglers in Yorkshire.

The situation was ideal for a keeny carper. Basically the owner Jim Whitfield didn't like night fishing. On several occasions Jim had said to me, "If you're not good enough to catch 'em during the day you don't deserve to catch 'em." Over two or three years, I became good friends with Jim, and eventually started to help out with a bit of weekend bailiffing, peg maintenance, etc.

In return Jim let me night fish, and to invite a mate to fish with me. That mate was Dave McMillan, and for two or three seasons we had permission to night fish, on a lake where night fishing was banned.

A very wild looking Brian, night stalking at Emmotland.

The Emmotland ponds were popular day ticket fisheries at this time. Those Emmotland fish took some pressure during the day, but were used to having it all their own way after dark. It was like inviting a chocoholic to be night security guard at Cadbury's.

Dave and I had some fabulous fishing, and during the summer months used to do a lot of night stalking. We noticed that on the warmer nights the fish would come right into the edges and feed on what anglers had thrown in as they left. Quite often we'd see anglers throw bits of sandwiches etc. into the lake. After everyone had gone, on the still nights, you could hear carp slurping on the scraps of bread. Dave and I hatched a plan, and it worked brilliantly. What we used to do, was keep an eye on the weather, till a hot still night was forecast. We would arrive just before dark, with a sliced loaf. Once everybody had packed up and gone, we'd walk round the lake, and throw a couple of slices in each swim. Set-up a soft rod, with fairly heavy line, and just tie a hook on the end. A few bits and pieces in a small bag, plenty of crust, then sit and listen. When you heard the slurping, quietly make your way to the area. Put on a large piece of crust, listen again for the slurp, gently lower the crust, and wait for the line to pull. When it did, strike, the water would erupt, and it was game on! Dave and I had as many as a dozen fish in a night like this, and the only way we would know where we were, was from the splashing of the hooked fish.

One night, the conditions were perfect. We arrived, and put out the sliced bread. It wasn't long before we heard the first slurp, then another.

"See you later, Dave..."

I slowly made my way into the peg where I thought the slurp had come from. I stood in the inky darkness and listened. Yes, there it was again. I made my way an inch at a time to the front of the peg. There it was again. I unhooked the hook from the side of the first rod-ring and double hooked the matchbox-sized bit of crust in place. I gently lowered the crust towards the water, until the lack of weight told me it was on the surface. Another slurp, and the pulse quickened, any second now. But it didn't happen. It went quiet, and I was about to give in and move on when I could just make out ripples coming from near my bread. A slight splash, any second now ...Yes, I can feel the line starting to tighten ...that's a definite movement ....strike!

At which point a bloody great rat shot out of the water into the air, looped over a branch directly above me, before landing on my head on the way down. I ducked and weaved like Mohammed Ali, trying to miss the rat, which was swinging back and forth. Eventually, I was able to give out a bit of line. I got Ratty into the landing net, at which point the barbless hook fell out, and the rat shot off, none the worse for wear.

Which is more than could be said for either my nerves, or my head.

Still in Yorkshire ....

A little bit further down the same chain of ponds is a water that used to be called Thompson's. It's now run as a very successful syndicate by Dave Laws. When I used to fish it, it was controlled by Hull and District Angling Association, and I had several good years on the water before moving on.

To reach the fishing areas on Thompson's you had to drive through a farm yard, and then along a track to the swims. You could fish most of one bank but the opposite side was out of bounds to fishing. At one end, just before the no fishing area, was a sign that always used to make me smile. It went something like, Can you run a mile in four minutes? ....The bull in this field can do it in three.

I never tested the claim!

The lake was basically two lakes joined by a narrow channel. One of my favourite swims was about midway down the first half, on a small piece of bank that jutted out slightly into the lake. It was a smallish peg, and it was a tight squeeze to get a bivvy and your rods into it. When everything was in position you

Success for Brian at Thompson's.

had a narrow space down the side of the bivvy, and your rod butts would be just inside your bivvy door.

It was a lovely peg, commanding a lot of water, and I had several good sessions in that peg, but one sticks in my mind for a different reason.

This particular day I'd squeezed my gear into position as usual. I'd got cast out, and spent a pleasant evening watching the water for fish, brewing tea, etc. All the things you do when you're on your own on a carp session. Some time after dark I checked my buzzers, and got in the bag, and fell asleep.

I was awake, I hadn't opened my eyes yet, but I could hear and feel breathing close to my face.

I was no longer alone in my bivvy!

I slowly opened my eyes ...It was a cow!

In the half-light of dawn, I was struggling to believe what was happening. Somehow this bloody great cow had come down the side of my bivvy, had stepped over my rods and was now stood with my rods between its legs, and its head in my bivvy door, trying to lick my face. It wasn't love at first sight!

What did I do? If I had moved, and the cow panicked I could have ended up with three piece instead of two piece rods. I couldn't just lie there ...It may have wanted to get even more friendly!

I very slowly rolled off the back of my sleeping bag so I was on the ground

The 'cow' swim at Thompson's.

between my bedchair, and the back of my brollie. Fortunately the overwrap I was using did not have a sewn in groundsheet, so I carefully slid my hand underneath the back corner, and worked the peg loose. All the while being watched by a very laid back Daisy. Once I'd got the peg out I was able to force the corner of the brollie up, and wriggle out ...commando style.

Once out, I was able to sneak up behind Daisy, who for some reason still had her head in my bivvy door.....probably trying to work out where the prat on the sleeping bag had disappeared to!

I carefully reached between Daisy's legs, for my rods, and moved them to the reeds at the side of the peg. I repeated the same process with the rod rests. Now all I had to do was remove the cow!

Over the years I've not done much with cows, and was at a bit of a loss. I tried getting a bunch of grass, and prodding it on the nose with it, but it wasn't impressed. I tried clapping my hands, it still wasn't impressed.

Just then my saviour arrived.... The farmer.

"Good morning," he said, "have you seen a cow?"

He looked over my shoulder, and a big grin, started to spread all over his face. Apparently one had escaped overnight from the holding pen. With an expert on hand Daisy was soon backed up, out of my peg, and led away.

"Thanks mate ....," I said, relieved, "I don't suppose you've got any spare milk?"

Resting Rocky ....
For many years I have been a member of a syndicate in Norfolk. Of all the waters I have ever fished, this Norfolk water will always be very special to me. Over the years I've had many memorable sessions there, and made many friends. It's a lovely water, very well run, with some immaculate fish.

For several years the owners had two Rottweilers. They were lovely dogs, Lucas and Rocky, but I think it's fair to say that at times they could be a little temperamental. I don't think I was the only syndicate member that was a little nervous of these two dogs. One had the reputation for being a little bit more short-tempered than the other, but I could never remember which, so in truth I treated both with a little caution.

Under normal circumstances their presence was not a problem. When any syndicate members were on site, they were kept well under control in a purpose made compound, but on this particular day, I fooled the system.

The owner's house was in one corner of the lake, and oversaw one of the main car parks. This car park gave access to one complete bank of the lake, which you reached by walking across the lawn in front of the house. The second car park was midway along the far bank, and was therefore used by those anglers fishing that bank, and the far end of the lake.

I was on holiday, and on a session of several days. I was fishing the far side of the lake, so was parked up in the second far car park. On this particular day, despite it being mid summer, the lake was virtually deserted, with only one other angler fishing, two pegs further down from me.

If I'm on a longish session, I often like to take a break from the main rods, and wander off to do a bit of surface fishing, or general stalking.

Come early afternoon, the wander-lust set in. So I set up a float rod, picked up a few bits and pieces, and went for a walk. I headed towards the bottom end of the lake, the area furthest away from the house. I spent some time sitting looking for fish, but couldn't spot anything special. It occurred to me that as the main car park was empty, one whole side of the lake would have been still and quiet all day. It was worth a walk back round the long way, to check out a few likely areas.

I slowly made my way back towards the main car park, on the bank opposite to where I was fishing, checking out potential swims. Bingo! Just when I thought I would draw a blank, I spotted some fish. Half a dozen, including a couple of twenties, in only a couple of feet of water. Close to the bank, and really grubbing up the bottom, this was a chance too good to miss. I set my float to about three feet, and slowly crept into the peg, a gentle underhand swing and the bait and float landed perfectly. I slowly placed the rod on the grass to my side, and turned the spool a few times to cock the float. I settled in the grass to await events, using a convenient tree as a backrest. As I sat there I started crumbling up a few boilies to occasionally flick around the float.

A lovely warm, still, summer's afternoon, relaxing in the sun .... when I heard the patter of doggy feet ....I slowly turned, and came face to face, literally, with a large Rottweiler. We eyed each other up, and "he" decided we would be good company for each other, as a few moments later he laid down beside me, resting his head on my knee.

I wondered where the owner was - I could guess what had happened. He would have looked out at an empty car park, and thought, I can let Rocky have a bit of a run. Quite a reasonable idea, except he wouldn't have known that some idiot from Yorkshire had gone walk-a-bout, the long way round.

At this point, the float dipped, and a small cloud of silt, puffed up just past it. I went to move. An angry lip curled up, as a slow menacing snarl, suggested that Rocky wasn't quite finished with his pillow.

Once again the float dipped, and I started to work out how much it would cost to replace the rod, once it had been towed in ...? 'cos sure as hell, I wasn't moving!

At this point the fish flicked its tail, decided it didn't want my bait, and moved off. My rod was safe for the moment. As I'd been walking round, I'd had a can of

The Norfolk syndicate also produced the goods for Brian.

coke, and as Rocky and I continued to sit in companionable silence, my bladder started to suggest some relief might be in order. An attempt to relieve the growing numbness in my bum was met with another snarl ...this was turning out to be the longest fifteen minutes stalking I'd ever done!

Just when things were reaching crisis proportions of numbness and bladder control, I heard the owner call Rocky. The relief when Rocky pricked up his ear, got up, shook himself, and headed for home, without a backward glance in my direction, was marginally greater than the relief a few seconds later, which took place against the nearest tree.

I collected my rod, and started walking back to my main fishing area. As I walked across the lawn, past the house, the owner saw me, and we exchanged pleasantries. He said he was surprised to see me, as he thought the bank was empty. I got the impression he was glad to see me in one piece ....

At least he didn't asked me, if I'd had any bites!

The How to Team put up a bivvy ....

Enough of animals ...Lets move on to one of the funniest moments in my angling memory banks.

Martyn, my son, and I had arrived about 5p.m. one Friday night, for a weekend session. It was a lovely summer's evening, we'd found a couple of pegs we fancied, and got set-up. Rods were cast, tea was brewed, we were chilling out.

A van approached along the track towards us, and stopped about 40yds away. Three guys got out and started unloading gear.

"Dad, are you watching this?"

I certainly was, but pretending I wasn't. This was going to be serious entertainment. From the van had come a bivvy, still in its sealed plastic bag, and various other overnight essentials, sleeping bags, and a giant inflatable mattress.

It was obvious that none of these guys had used any of this gear before, and they weren't into instruction manuals either.

One guy found a foot pump, moved to one side away from the other two, connected the pipe, and started stamping up and down, on the pump, to inflate the air-bed ..... two hours to dark, he might just make it!

Back to the main show .... By now we have various elasticated poles assembled, and we are trying to work out which pole goes in which sleeve. Now it might be obvious that the two main cross-over poles will be the same length, but not to these guys. It took an awful lot of F'in this, and F'in that, before we had the three poles in the right sleeves, and the inner tent upright.

Pump Man was still going strong on the mega air-bed.

The inner tent was now being positioned in front of the swim, and the mallet was out to help peg it down.

"Dad, dad ....the door's at the back."

"Martyn those three guys are bigger than us. Stop laughing, and look away."

The air-bed is starting to take shape!

The outer skin is unfolded, and the two guys, one at each end, are approaching the inner tent. It is thrown over the inner tent, this time with the door facing the swim, and again thoroughly pegged down.

The air-bed is up, and being tested for pressure ....nearly there!

"Dad ..how are they going to get the air-bed in the bivvy?"

"Shut up, stop laughing, or we'll end up in casualty!"

Back to the bivvy team. One approaches the bivvy, and unzips the door. There is a pause, a discussion, a look in our direction, and they start to walk over.

That's it ...they've heard us laughing, we're dead!

They reach our peg ... we try to look serious ... intent on our fishing.

"Hello mate," said Bivvy Man One.

"Caught owt?" asked Bivvy Man Two.

"You wouldn't believe this," said Bivvy Man One. "We've paid good money for a brand new bivvy, and they've sold us one without an F'in inside door!"

Martyn must have choked on something, as he sort of got a fit of coughing. I offered expressions of sympathy, and managed to suggest that they might have the inner tent the wrong way round.

They went back to Pump Man who had just completed total inflation.

The outer tent was unpegged and removed. I was given the thumbs up, and the inner tent was unpegged, and turned round .....both were pegged down again, a successful erection was complete.

Pump Man picks up the giant air-bed, and approaches the bivvy.

"Dad, Dad ....it won't go in!"

"Don't look!"

Lots of pushing, bending, stretching, and Martyn is proved right ....it won't go in!

You could almost see the tears, on Pump Man's face, as he reached to unscrew the release valve....

The Steaming Crotch

It's back to the syndicate water in Norfolk again. I had gained permission for Bill Cottam to join me for a few days in early November, for a four day session.

It's my experience that fishing in November can either be very good, or a total disaster. The biggest single factor being the weather. It's the time of year when you can get wide variations in weather. If it's mild and muggy, overcast or showery, wet and windy, I'm OK, any of those I can cope with. However, I hate the high pressures that bring with them the crystal clear skies, and the first severe frosts of the winter. It's my experience, that they can totally knock the fishing on the head, and my confidence plunges with the thermometer.

I'd really been looking forward to this session, and was counting the days, but as the session neared, the high pressure system took hold, and the areas of blue started to appear on the weather map. The first frosts of the winter were on their way!

Bill and I met up at the lake and had a look round. Two pegs were selected next to each other, midway between two islands. Gear was trolleyed, bivvies sorted, rods assembled etc. and by mid-afternoon we were fishing. It was sunny, warm, not a cloud in the sky, but by six it was dark, cold, and getting colder. We sat outside the bivvy, watching our breath cloud the night air. The moon was full and bright, the stars shone brightly, and twinkled on the growing frost patches around where we were fishing ...oh sod it!

Catching fish in these conditions might be a problem, but at least I had a secret weapon in the struggle to stay warm ....Boots' hot chocolate!

Unfortunately they've stopped making it, but take my word for it, it was superb.

Putting two extra spoonfuls in the mug, produced this rich milky hot chocolate, that you could almost feel warming you up. As the temperatures continued to plummet, it was time for the hot choc ....they became an instant hit with Bill, and several were consumed before we retired to our bivvies.

No fish were caught overnight ...surprise, surprise! There was a severe frost, no surprise!

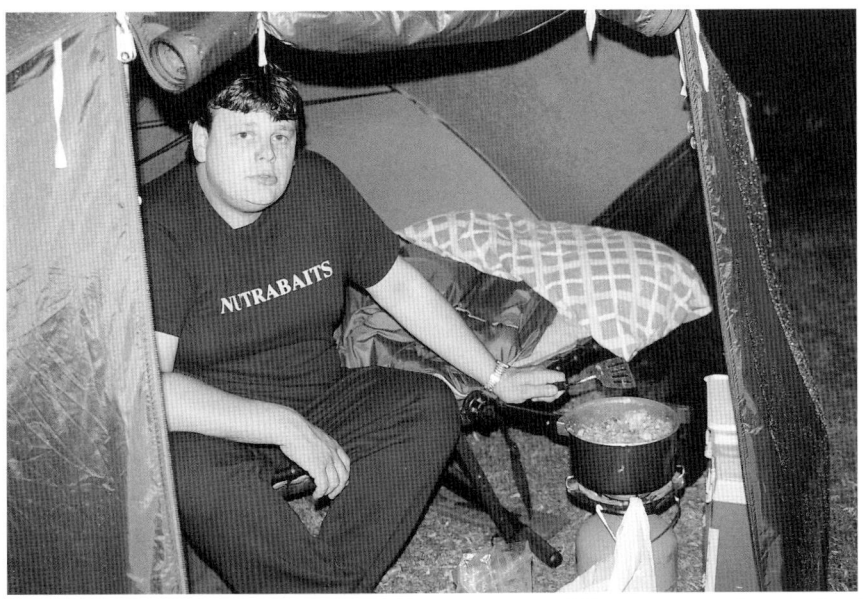

Big Bill cooking up a storm at Norfolk just to prove he was there!

Mid morning we popped to the local supermarket, and Bill knowing how to live suggested a mark two hot choc. Hot choc, with cream. Sounded good to me, so a can of cream was put into the trolley. We knew how to live in those days

The second night was a repeat of the first, except it felt even colder. The hot chocolate with cream was the highlight. I did manage a small mirror overnight, but that was it.

Our bivvies were about 20yds apart, and we'd got into the habit of sitting midway between, easy to get to either set of rods, and still have a natter.

Day three passed without event, and again as the sun disappeared, so the moon appeared, the stars shone, and the frost bit deep.

"Fancy a hot chocolate?"

"Go on then."

I got up from where we were sitting, put the kettle on, and counted six spoonfuls into each mug. As the steam poured from the kettle I stirred the mix until both mugs were full. Then a generous squirt of cream on top.

I walked them over to where Bill was sitting, put them on the ground between the chairs, and went back for a packet of biscuits. I was just about to turn back when I heard Bill ....make some comment. I turned, took in the scene, and burst out laughing.

In picking up the mug, it had obviously slipped. In the moonlight, I could see most of the contents of a mug of hot chocolate, plus a generous helping of cream, resting very peacefully in the lap of Bill's one piece thermal suit.

The memory of that scene, has cracked me up many times since, as in the moonlight, the steam drifted into the air...

Bill just sat back, and with perfect timing, sighed and said ...

"Oh, I did enjoy that!"

I just wished I'd had the presence of mind to take a picture, but in truth I wouldn't have been able to hold the camera still anyhow.

That's it then, some of my Carp Tales. I've been aware as I've sat at the PC, that I've often been laughing to myself as I've been typing. It's been great fun writing this, I just hope you get as much enjoyment from reading about them too.

Have fun, as you live your own Carp Tales.

Dawn at the Norfolk syndicate lake.

I wish I didn't have to remember!

by Julian Cundiff

Was it only '98 when I last contributed to the first Carp Tales book? It seems so long ago and the stories even more so. Mind you a lot can happen in three years and in my case has. A change in my domestic circumstances has meant that I've had to relearn the art of foreplay once again and even up date my Brut and Blue Stratos aftershave collection - such is life. Mind you, it does mean I can cover one or two of my more memorable exploits (nothing to do with fishing of course) without the fear of Julie putting one of Nashy's rod rests where the sun doesn't shine...ouch! Sorry love, it all happened before I met you so please forgive me if you can.

Don't make love in the dark.
Quite some years ago I met and fell head over heels in love with an absolute cracker called Kate. For six months even carp fishing took a back seat to this apparition of blond hair and leather and all seemed rosy in the garden. Hell, I even intended to fly us to the USA for a New Jersey wedding where we'd have been rigged up in the full Bon Jovi gear. Now all you young trendies may well laugh, but back in 1988 Bon Jovi were the boys and even my hairstyle seemed logical...sort of! However, like true shooting stars we exploded rather than faded away and I was a single man once again. Mind you, Tim Paisley did tell me that as soon as he saw her he knew she'd do some damage to me - dead right, Tim.

Back on the prowl and by hook or by crook I ended up dating the YTS trainee at the court at the time. Out of courtesy I won't use her real name but I was pretty sure she was 16, mind you I was 26! I must admit I wasn't back into my fishing mode but couldn't resist the odd visit to the lakes with 'J' to see how my mates were getting on. My fishing partner at the time, Mark, was even more of a ladies' man than I could ever hope to be, so he always encouraged me to bring my 'friends' down to see him. Only in later years did I find out that he tried to chat most of them up. Good work, fellah! Down to the lake in the half-light and we walked round the lake hand in hand (sickly, I know, but sixteen year olds love it) to see Mark. Approaching his swim from the left I could see he was set up and fishing and the carp sack hanging in the trees revealed he'd already caught. As I stood in the doorway of his shelter and chatted carp, carp, carp, poor old 'J' stood behind me trying to look interested - not! Eventually enough was enough for poor old 'J' and as if to encourage me to move on a dainty little hand crept round and reached into my trouser pocket at the front.

Now poor old Mark nearly had a thrombosis looking at that and his eyes were on stalks at the sight. Needless to say I did take the hint from 'J' and said to Mark, "We will just have a look further down, mate," and off we went to his right. By now it was pitch black and with all the trees around the lake you really couldn't see a thing. I think 'J's hormones had gone into overdrive, like they do when you are sixteen, and three swims down she suggested we sit down for a cuddle. Well, who was I to deny her that? So, off came my jacket and cuddle we did. As any red-blooded male will know a cuddle led to other things and in just a short time a frantic parting of clothes and energetic and very loud lovemaking session took place. Who needs carp fishing? I'd like to say that half an hour later we reclothed and moved on but you'd all call me a liar and you'd probably be right. So ten minutes later feeling all hot and

"In the half light I thought we were alone."

blustered we straightened up our clothes, made ourselves half-presentable and carried on back to the car. Unfortunately due to the cloak of darkness and enthusiasm of 'J' I'd not checked for fellow anglers on the lake and literally ten feet from our scene of passion was a poor old float angler watching his glowing Starlite (ow, er, missus!). I hadn't seen him at the time and even worse he was the club secretary at the time. As we walked past him he didn't flinch or move a muscle and you could almost see his knuckles turning white as he gripped the rod. What could I say? What could we say? Nothing, I suppose, and two embarrassed lovers trotted off back to the car the long way round. Funnily enough that swim ended up being called the 'somebody's coming' swim and whenever I see the old lad he still winks at me!

A long way to go for a sausage roll
Although I'd enjoyed my time on my local lakes I really felt the need to spread my wings a little and see if the Promised Land down south was paved with gold and carp as the magazines portrayed it. Unfortunately I was still carless which served me right for only dating girls with cars, so any trips south of Watford would have to be with my old mate, Eric Hodson a.k.a. Uncle Backstop. We'd both read every issue of Carp Fisher and scanned the weeklies and in the mid-eighties it seemed the only place to catch a really big carp was the Yateley complex in Hampshire. At that time permits were very easy to obtain and after a telephone call of enquiry and writing the relevant cheques out, our permits arrived. Yateley, you can get ready...idiots! First trip was planned for mid-August, which was probably as hopeless a time as you could pick but for two northern bumpkins it seemed to make sense. We'd had an excellent start at the Tilery with carp to almost thirty pounds so a forty would do nicely thank you - titter you not. I was put in charge of bait and tackle and good old Eric was put in charge of food, transport and selecting which lake we would catch our forty on. Funnily enough when I suggested to Eric that 30 cheese slices, a dozen bread rolls, some Snackpots and digestive biscuits would do us the week, he decided to take over the cooking side of our trip. Bait wise I'd stocked up on Hutchy's new ready mades which I can't for the life of me remember what they were but they smelt like a woman's perfume and were as soft as old Selman's tummy.

Uncle Eric likes to take the kitchen sink.

Gary Dennis recommended them to me but bearing in mind

That's Ross, notice he's well behind me in case of a cyanide special.

he lives in Lincolnshire and they all seem to marry their sisters what chance did I have? Although I'd got the permits sorted out with Eric's connections down south in the BCSG and Saga I left him to select the lake and swim...mmmm! First trip would be a Monday to Friday trip so Eric motored over to my house on the Sunday so we could make an early start on Monday. When I say "my house" I mean my parents' house of course but luckily enough they did spend a lot of time away so I could come and go as I pleased. Mind you, I always used to tell the girlies it was my house which worked when they were young enough not to know any better! 3a.m. and the alarm's going mad and by 4a.m. Eric, Ross and myself are on the way to the capital of the carp-fishing world. Ross being Eric's faithful dog that went everywhere with him and also wore a shirt and tie like Eric! Poor old Eric's 240 Volvo groaned under the weight of us all as it spluttered along the M1 towards the Promised Land. Now Eric was a lovely chap but he did have this habit of forgetting he was in fourth until I reminded him to put it into fifth. No wonder he only got twenty to the gallon out of it! So what should have been a four-hour trip maximum ended up as almost six hours and when you are sat with a dog with an extreme flatulence problem it's no fun. Poor old Eric's sense of smell had deserted him so Ross's cyanide specials didn't affect him at all; I just sat and died. By 10a.m. we were almost there and the famous signs kept flashing into view. Sandhurst, Yateley, Camberley ...we were there!

Into the car park and out I fell. The aroma of Eric's pipe and Ross's cyanide specials crept out with me and leaves on surrounding trees started to fall off - yuk. Amazingly there was only one other car at the complex so we didn't need to rush to find a swim to say the least. Instead we decided to find the nearest sandwich shop and have something to eat; funnily enough my stomach felt a little queasy so I decided to keep it to a small meal. A quick stroll into Yateley and we found a nice little baker's where we stocked up on bread, milk and sausage rolls. Now it's time to catch a forty - like you do! Back into the car park and a third car had joined us and looking at the sticker in his car and the badge on the bloke's jacket he was a bailiff. After the usual introductions and a check of our permits, our bailiff friend pointed to Ross and reminded us that dogs are not allowed. What! Not his rule, of course, but he had to administer it and if Ross stayed we'd end up losing our permits. Oh no, please tell me this isn't happening? What could we do? I couldn't bump poor Ross off and I didn't want to set up to be banned. We only had one choice and it didn't sit very well. We had to go home that day. A quick camera shot of the complex and away we went. Almost twelve hours of travelling in one day - a hell of a long way to go for a sausage roll and a cup of coffee, I can tell you. And just to add insult to injury I left my damn camera on the fence at Yateley when I locked the gate. Mind you it was a horrible Zenith that was near impossible to focus with properly. So whoever found it...good luck, keep it!

F-f-f-frozen

In a day and age when we seem to take cars for granted I can remember that during most of the eighties I had to rely on a pushbike, moped or, in the mid-eighties, a good old Honda XL185 four stroke motorbike. Looking at the tackle I take nowadays I find it hard to believe I could carry all the gear on the bike. With a rod bag flailing all over the show like a demented helicopter blade, a rucksack on my back guaranteed to throw me off at the first tight corner and bait bucket hanging off each side of the handle bars I'm amazed the police didn't stop me more often. It certainly wasn't down to speed as I could barely hit 55mph on the bike so outrunning a police car was unlikely unless we went cross-country. For local trips it wasn't too bad as circulation only seemed to get cut off after 10 minutes or so. No matter how I arranged the rucksack straps I never could avoid the circulation problem and inevitably I'd have to pull in, unload, shake my arms until the feeling came back and then carry on. You lot don't know how easy you've got it nowadays.

Unfortunately my local lakes didn't allow close season fishing so full of carp fever I had to travel a little further afield to satisfy my yearnings. Luckily a lake around twenty miles away at Tyram Hall did allow any method trout fishing and as it held a good stock of singles and doubles if the trout didn't pick up my Richworth Salmon Supreme maybe a carp would. Of course I wouldn't actually be fishing for carp but if a lovely 8 ounce trout won't pick up a hair rigged boilee and a carp does instead that's not my fault, is it? I just love catching half-pound trout...honestly! Early April and my first trip was planned, just a day trip to see if it really was as good as the publicity said it was. The weather had been really kind and most days were comparatively hot and sunny, maybe not ideal for catching carp but nice to idle away time fishing for carp in.

6a.m. and I'm loaded up and put-putting my way to the water. Even as I left my house it felt warm and it was fully daylight and clearly a good one at that. By 7a.m., I was at the lake after a leisurely drive and ready to catch some carp, whoops, I mean trout! Bait at the time was Richworth's stunning Salmon Supreme boilies or chopped luncheon meat held on with a sliver of grass. By 12noon I'd had two nice double figure mirrors and a common a tad under ten. Despite the early promise of a good day the sky had clouded up somewhat and a chilly wind was starting to bite even with the good old Steadfast 45" brolly behind me. This wasn't the plan. By 3p.m. it didn't look nice at all and the cloud had a horrible grey tinge to it...a tinge that reminded me of snow - gulp! Time to pack up I thought, maybe I could get a slight refund on my day ticket. Old Selman would be proud of me. With the limited amount of tackle I had I was packed up and on the road in less than twenty minutes, but unfortunately it looked horrendous. I'd only brought a silly, little, thermal, grey, posing jacket with me and my waterproofs hadn't left the tackle shed at home - dumbo! My lightweight Moto-X gloves may well impress the girlies but had all the thermal properties of an ice cube as my fingertips could testify...if I could feel them that is. Snowflakes started to batter my face to such an extent that I had to drop the visor to protect my eyes. Within a minute the visor would steam up like the back window of a courting couple's car so I had to open it up for more pain. By now the thermal jacket was sodden and I really started to feel unwell as the flakes turned into a full-blown snowstorm. I was only seven odd miles from home but it felt like eternity. Not only was I cold, I felt I was dying. Whilst trying to wipe my visor with a dead hand, I lost a bait bucket from the handlebar, sod it - keep it. The large, black, Hutchy rucksack felt like the devil on my back and the swaying rod holdall made me look like a helicopter in its death throes. Help! Luckily I made it home without a serious accident, God knows how. The tackle was literally left where it fell and the bike abandoned against the house wall. Shaking like Selman when he's asked to get a round in, I literally crawled up the stairs to the bathroom to the hot bath my mother had run. That's the last any method trout fishing I do in April I can tell you.

Motorway Mammeries

After a successful 20 x 20's at the Tilery I really didn't fancy a step backwards so instead decided to spend a year at Hull and District's fabled Motorway Pond available on the same ticket. Named due to its proximity to the M62 motorway the water was a hotch potch of mini lakes joined together and was full of snags and carp. Best fish in the water were big twenties and growing and with a number of good back up fish it really looked appealing to me. Although you could fish either water on one Hull night permit generally each lake had its own fans with the Tilery lads and the Motorway lads keeping themselves to themselves. Something of a rivalry had grown up and each team had its own T-shirts to wear. Tilery had its "Night on the Tiles" shirt and Motorway its "Motorway Madness" one. Believe me these boys took it very seriously indeed - stop tittering at the back Mr. Gibbons and Mr. Skoyles! As an outsider to both Tilery and Motorway I'd not been granted the ultimate accolade of a T-shirt but I didn't find it affected my run rate too much. Because I didn't know too much about the Motorway Lake I did spend quite some time walking its banks and looking for signs of its fabled fish. Although I did find quite a few fish in the usual spots they certainly were not the big fish I was after and after a frustrating month of catching lots of bream and some double figure carp I decided to pull off for a week to rethink and regroup. This seemed to do the trick as two evenings' observation taught me more than one month of fishing had done.

Some very, very large carp were definitely patrolling round a large weedbed out from Rat Island and I was pretty convinced that the fish I had seen crashing was the one the lads had imaginatively titled "The Big 'Un". Unfortunately two trips to Rat Island showed me that the weed in front of it made landing carp almost impossible and one carp landed and one lost was not my sort of ratio. Opposite Rat Island was a swim called Thomo's Point named after the larger than life Geoff Thompson who had fished it time and time again when the water first came under Hull and District AA's control. This turned out to be an ideal swim to cast across to Rat Island from and within the first seven days I'd notched up a cracking 30.04 and 29.00; that went down well with a number of the locals...NOT! Luckily Geoff Thompson didn't fall into that narrow-minded stance and took the time to visit me and congratulate me on my success. He even promised me a Motorway Madness T-shirt; forget the lottery. Now Geoff has always been one for the ladies and with his perma tan, gold chains and John Wayne walk couldn't seem to go wrong. Don't you just hate blokes who have 24-7 suntans? Anyway at this stage he'd pulled an absolute cracker who had a natural 40FF chest so he assured me. I'd seen the lady in question and didn't doubt him in the slightest but I must admit I'd never seen such a naturally occurring phenomenon myself. Jokingly I told Geoff I'd be more impressed with a T-shirt if she was in it....

Twenty four hours later and I'm back in the same swim on an overnighter once again when good old Geoff appears with the lady in question! Whilst I'm not one to be embarrassed easily I knew she knew what I'd said to Geoff and to be fair I felt a little bit red round the face. Certainly the lady seemed to be all Geoff claimed she was...

"Have you got your camera, Jules?"

"Of course, Geoff, but why do you ask?"

"Because .... is going to give you a picture of her in a Motorway Madness T-shirt."

Geoff had the T-shirt in his hand so I didn't doubt him and who am I to argue with him? So I went to the rucker and got my camera bag out. At the very least I expected the lady to be a little bit embarrassed and get changed out of sight - not this one. In full sight of cars whizzing down the M62 and not three feet in front of me she took off her jersey and bra to reveal...plain old flesh but so beautifully crafted. Lordy, lordy I've gone to heaven! To be honest I didn't know what to say when she uttered the immortal words, "How do you want me?" No words came out. Eventually I did regain my composure and managed to rattle off a few 'big brace' shots in both Motorway Madness T-shirt and my good old Daiwa jacket. Needless to say the swim has become renowned for its big brace and I never did get to keep the T-shirt! Mind you Geoff didn't manage to keep the girl, which was probably a good thing as she'd been through three husbands when she met him!

40 plus!

Barrow hell

For years and years I was always a one tripper man when it came to carrying fishing tackle and in my own words, "Barrows are for wimps." However, with the ever-increasing amount of tackle I carry and the quality of barrows even I had to admit defeat and decided that if you can't beat 'em you might as well join 'em. Now a properly loaded, fully functioning barrow is an item of joy and I agree is an absolute godsend to today's modern carp angler. However, barrows have one major problem - bleedin' punctures when you least want one. You never get a puncture close to the car; it's always at the swim especially when the swim is miles from the car. Forget solid tyres, they rattle more than a granny at an Anne Summers party. Love 'em or hate 'em....

I'd arranged a session at Catch 22 with good mates Brian Skoyles and Glyn Leach. Now Catch 22 provide their own barrows and top quality ones at that. Fully strengthened, pneumatic tyres and straps built in, marvellous! Arriving at the car park at first light I was amazed to see the far nature reserve swims free so onto the barrow went all the tackle and off trotted Jules and Glyn. Now I must admit that the tyre did feel a little soft at the time but I put it down to the sheer amount of tackle and mucky books I had with me. I once made the mistake of telling Spug and Co I did like to see the odd naked lady picture now and again and ever since then I have been inundated with reading of a fairly pictorial nature. Twenty-four hours in the swim produced absolutely zilch and it was clear to both Glyn and myself that the lake was definitely out of sorts. A clear blue sky didn't inspire me either, so we decided to cut our trip short and concentrate on a more local lake instead. All the tackle was fastidiously loaded onto the barrow and away I went. Unfortunately my soft tyre had gone from soft to flaccid and was as flat as a fart so to speak. Now I know the obvious thing would be to walk back to the car park, get another barrow and walk back to my swim and reload it once again. Call me a pratt but I wasn't going to be beaten by a barrow and I really didn't fancy any extra trips or unloading sorties. Already perched on top of the trolley were four large, white bait buckets, two Stacksacks, a Titan rod holdall, a large bedchair bag, waders and porn bag. Come on Jules, it isn't that far...is it? With the wet ground underfoot it didn't feel too bad at first as the barrow sort of slid along like a sledge in the snow. However, this was because I was fresh as a daisy, young, drunk and full of you know what! But having

Revenge on Brian at last.

completed 2oo yards and with twice that to complete it started to go horribly wrong. For a start I was overheating in my Nashy undersuit and the pushing really was taking its toll on me. Blisters were starting to appear on my powder puff office worker hands and my heart was pounding like there was no tomorrow. To make things worse I could see Brian Skoyles had arrived, was set up in the car park swim all of ten feet from his car and, watching through binoculars, he was obviously revelling in my pain...as I would have done if the boot had been on the other foot. Or should that be if the puncture had been on the other barrow? 200 yards to go and I could taste blood in my mouth and my head felt like someone had stuck it in the bass bin at a Motorhead concert. I know I should have done some smaller journeys but I was determined not to be beaten especially in front of the grinning Brian and Martyn. Won't give in, won't give in...pratt, pratt, pratt! 100 yards to go and I'm shot. My knees were buckling and my heart going ten to the dozen. I was coughing up spittle red in colour and the swine in the car park were blatantly laughing at me. Help...50 yards to go and it might as well have been 500 or 5000. I was literally pushing and sliding the barrow in 5-yard bursts and I'm sure someone kept moving the car park further away. Finally, I collapsed in the car park much to the amusement of Bri, Martyn and Glyn. Told you I wouldn't be beaten - mind you I wasn't ready to drive back home for almost an hour either....Pride cometh before a heart attack I'm told.

Enjoy it, live it and remember things have got to get better...haven't they?

Carp tales comedy

Tony Miles

Cuttle Mill Mayhem
Probably the funniest incident I've seen in my carp fishing career occurred at Cuttle Mill in the late seventies. It was before the drawing lots for swim system, but more a first past the post race for swims. One of the most popular areas at the time was the bank facing the house across the lake, where a shortish cast put your bait near to the bed of lilies, and an angler raced round there at breakneck speed one early morning. All he was carrying were two rod rests and two made up rods, already baited.

Having triumphantly got the swim he wanted, he immediately proceeded to put out his two hook baits, before then taking a leisurely stroll back to the car for the rest of his gear. Quite why he had to put the baits out straight away I shall never know. It was illegal in any event, leaving the rods unattended like that, but the angler concerned was soon to pay for his misdemeanour.

He was perhaps twenty yards away from the rods on his return, laden down as he was with all the paraphernalia of the modern carper, when his right hand alarm sounded. No sooner had that occurred when the rod took off and sailed into the lake like a Polaris missile. Obviously, he had neglected to check that his reel was on free spool, as these were the days before bait runners. As he started to run, all his luggage became dangerously unstable, and the next moment there was a terrific splash as he tripped over his bedchair and took a gambol into the lake. Laughter echoed from all corners of the fishery.

Eventually, he sorted himself out, and it was now time to retrieve the rod. The corks were visible just short of the lilies. The carp was long gone, and our hero was muttering and swearing as he eventually waded back to shore and clambered onto the bank. Moments later, the second rod did exactly the same disappearing act! This time, he was right beside his tackle, but he was still too late. His despairing dive missed the fast escaping rod butt and he did another impressive belly flop into the lake. By now, everyone around the water was crying!

When the angler involved had eventually retrieved his second rod, again minus carp, he packed his gear up and went. I reckon he was on the bank less than twenty minutes in total, but what an impressive performance. The rest of that day turned out to be one of my best ever at the Mill. As well as a dozen doubles to 16lb, the hilarity on the bank that day made it an unforgettable experience.

Tony with a Cuttle Mill common.

The Crow

Napton reservoir, near Coventry, was the scene of some of my earliest angling exploits in the late sixties, and when the Coventry Specimen Group was up and running in 1967 we decided that Napton needed a few carp. Irksome details like actually asking for stocking permission were conveniently overlooked and quite a few stockies went in from an unfished farm pond over the next couple of seasons.

By the late seventies, fish to over 20lb were being caught, and Trefor and I decided on a two day session to see if we could nail one. On the afternoon of the second day, a scorching affair in mid July, all the carp were cruising around on the surface, taking wind blown insects as if they were born again trout. Off came the bottom baits, and out went two surface crusts, one anchored and one free to drift into surface lilies to my left.

Presently, two big carp were circling around the anchored bait fished at about fifty yards, and my eyes were focused intently on this activity. I was, therefore, startled when the alarm on the drifter rod suddenly screamed. Line was disappearing off the spool at an alarming rate. As soon as I picked up the rod I could sense there was something wrong. For a start, the line went straight up in the air, instead of into the water!

As the line tightened, another strange phenomenon occurred. Fifty yards above my head, a crow was flying backwards! There was no easy solution, the bird had to be brought down before we could release it, but that was easier said than done. If you've ever tried to stop a carrion crow flying at full pelt you'll know what I mean. It gives a whole new meaning to kite flying.

Eventually, the bird gave up the struggle and went into a steep dive, to land with a horrendous splash about twenty yards out. What happened next was quite astonishing. As if by magic, water birds of every description appeared, as if from nowhere. There were grebes, moorhens, pochards, tufties and mallards, plus others I didn't recognise. Within a few seconds, I swear there were over fifty attacking the helpless crow. There is no doubt they recognised it for what it was, a murderer of young chicks and a stealer of eggs. What goes around comes around, and they waded in with all fists flying, figuratively speaking.

It was perhaps four minutes or so before Trefor was able to net the now ravaged corpse, and it was indeed a chastening sight. It had been pecked to pieces. Napton's water fowl had exacted a terrible revenge on one of their greatest enemies.

The Great Storm
In the early days of the Coventry Specimen Group, we all devoted a lot of time to Marlborough Pool in Oxfordshire. My regular carping companion at the time was Mick Jelfs, now sadly deceased, and Mick and I were to share a truly terrifying experience in 1969. We had arrived on Friday evening for our usual 36 hour session, and by about midnight, the sky was lit with almost constant lightening, the wind was howling, and the rain ferocious. In my angling life, it still remains the most intense thunderstorm I've ever sat through.

There was nothing we could do but hang on and attempt to keep dry, easier said than done under a 36 inch umbrella surrounded by flimsy polythene, all that passed for a shelter in those days. By perhaps 1.00am the rain had eased a little, but the thunder and lightening were now occurring at the same instant, confirming that the epicentre was right overhead.

And then Mick shouted, "What the hell's that?"

As I looked up, I could see a rapidly growing ball of fire heading straight at us. In a panic, I dived off my chair to my right, just as I heard Mick do likewise. A second later, there was a terrifying whoosh and then a thunderous explosion right behind us. I don't mind admitting that it frightened the life out of me!

The next morning, sun now shining, Mick and I examined the grass behind the low bushes immediately behind the swim we were sharing. There, barely fifty feet from where we'd been sitting, was a scorch mark some ten yards across. A thunderbolt obviously, and had it been on a trajectory just a fraction different, it would have wiped the pair of us out that night.

Merv the Maggot

One of my longest standing and dearest friends in angling is Merv Wilkinson, one of the founder members of the Coventry Group with me. Although not specially interested in carp, Merv had a few sessions with us at Marlborough and one night can bring tears to my eyes even now.

Merv and Phil Smith were fishing a swim together called The Beach, where a sloping sandy bank led down to a lovely secluded bay, with rushes to the left and lilies to the right, a favourite haunt of carp at night. Merv and Phil were well away in the early hours. For those too young to remember carping in the sixties, the only bed chairs you could buy were those flimsy affairs from supermarkets sold for sunbathing. They were not very robust, rarely lasting more than a season, and had a disconcerting habit of either the thin walled aluminium tubing legs collapsing or folding flat with little provocation. Rolling over in your sleep could have some interesting side effects!

All was quiet, and then Merv's alarm was screaming as something took off across the bay. Startled, Merv tried to jump to his feet, but couldn't as he was zipped in his sleeping bag. In vain, he wrestled with the zip, which he soon found was jammed solid, and his contortions then led to the bedchair collapsing in a heap. On the ground and still trapped, writhing around like a giant maggot, he slowly rolled down the sandy slope into the margins. We were now nearly hysterical with laughter, but Merv was a sight to behold. Renowned for having a short fuse even on a good day, he was in an apoplexy of rage, roaring and swearing. The harder he struggled, the more comical it became.

Of course, Trefor put the tin hat on it. When Merv eventually stood on the bank, still in a foul mood, Trefor said,

"Merv, when you feel like getting that angry again, just whistle for a few minutes to calm down."

Merv nearly exploded.

"How the f*** can I whistle with f****** false teeth," he said, and promptly threw his teeth into the lake!

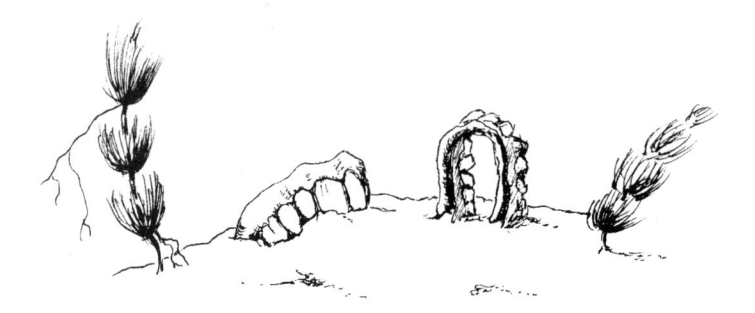

The Vixen
Another interesting session at Marlborough also centred round the dreaded supermarket bedchair.

Until 1970, most of our carp had fallen to either legered flake or floating crust, but special baits were slowly coming in to prominence, particularly Kit-E-Kat paste and some proprietary meat/biscuit meal concoctions. I had purchased some particularly fatty luncheon meat, and quickly found that the damn stuff floated. Those were the days when carp baits were either on the top or the bottom, not in between, so it never occurred to me to fish a popped up carp bait. Daft, really, as I'd caught plenty of big chub on popped up bread, in the shape of legered crust. Anyway, I decided to fish a large lump of floating meat, anchored near the Norfolk reeds with which Marlborough abounded. One area in the right hand corner of the lake had a lot of carp activity in late evening and I set up shop there for the dark hours. The problem was that the swim was extremely tight, with hardly any room for anyone to walk past. There was certainly no way I could erect an umbrella, but, as it promised a fine, clear night, I wasn't unduly worried. Just before dark, I positioned two anchored floaters, and then settled back on my bed chair. I had to remain as still as possible. There was quite deep water in the margins at this point, about four feet, and the carp came in close. Everything I might need during the dark hours was stowed under the bed, so that I could reach it easily without having to get up. The bait box holding my luncheon meat was among those items, but I could not have closed the lid properly.

At some time in the early hours, I woke up very uneasily. You know the feeling. Your eyes suddenly snap open, and you're not sure whether you heard something or whether you dreamt it. Suddenly, there was a thump in the small of my back, and then a vixen screamed. That's a blood curdling sound at the best of times, but when it happens two feet away in the dead of night, it's a case of breaking out the brown trousers. Anyway, I sat bolt upright in fright, and at that precise moment the animal dashed from under the chair, and then the front legs gave up the ghost. Seconds later, I had shot down the chair straight into four feet of cold water, just like a burial at sea.

One moment you're warm and snug in a sleeping bag, the next your thrashing around in cold water up to your neck. It doesn't half concentrate the mind!

That was the same session where I had travelled with Phil Smith, in his car. Phil and I have been friends for many years and he was always known for being, shall we say, careful with money. The example I'm about to relate is my favourite. On the second afternoon of the two day session, it got very hot and I had run out of drink. Suffering from thirst, I wandered round to Phil to see if I could scrounge some water, to find that he had a full bottle of lemonade unopened. Without hesitation, Phil cracked open the bottle and poured half the contents into my empty water bottle. A bottle of lemonade in 1970 would be about a shilling in old money, or 12 old pence, equivalent to 5p now.

When we eventually arrived at my front door after the session, I unloaded my gear and then asked Phil what I owed him for petrol. I have never forgotten his reply. He said, "Well, I've used four gallons, so you owe me for two gallons of petrol, plus sixpence for half a bottle of lemonade!"

An Awesome Battle
Still at Marlborough, and a story of my only true winter carp session. I remember Kevin Maddocks writing that he'd found Marlborough a good winter water, and that fired me to have a go in the mid eighties, in the company of my teenage son Chris. I was having grave doubts about the decision as I moved my gear round the lake. We'd had a severe frost, and freezing fog chilled me to the bone. Still, the forecast had promised long spells of winter sunshine later, and it would make a pleasant change from my usual chubbing.

Once I had reached the swim I fancied, I could barely see twenty yards, but could see enough to identify ice margins reaching out from the bank for at least fifteen of them. A steady ripple told me there was clear water beyond. Soon, I had propelled two strawberry cream boilies into the gloom, and Chris and I broke out the tea making tackle.

All was peaceful for about an hour and then a steady easterly wind got up, blowing left to right. At about the same time, my right hand alarm sounded, the bobbin dropped from the line and line began to coil off the spool. It was a strange slow run, and when I struck it was like hitting a brick wall. Nothing I did had any effect at all, line was taken steadily from the clutch whatever I did. When some forty yards had been taken, slowly but irresistibly, I started to lose patience and really crammed on the pressure. This certainly slowed down the rate of line loss, but didn't stop it. But what the extra pressure did do was produce some very curious creaking noises in the lake, and I peered through the rapidly clearing mist to try and make sense of it all. As the wind suddenly picked up force, the remaining mist cleared rapidly, and then the power of the run intensified. At that moment, everything suddenly became clear. I'd actually cast over an ice floe initially, about twenty feet square, and the wind had got this floe moving, eventually catching my line. I'd just spent twenty minutes playing a bloody block of ice!

Ice floes really scrap!

More Night Madness

Night fishing for carp, relying on alarms to wake you, often from a deep sleep, is a recipe for potential disaster. Jumping to your feet with a start leads to temporary disorientation, at which time anything can happen. I've had several funny moments.

In 1992, I had one of my best summers at a Midlands syndicate water, taking a good number of twenties, and one of the peculiarities of that particular summer was the constant north east wind, that seemed to be with us for weeks. One of my favourite swims was one called The Point, a very tight little swim where you just about had room to erect an umbrella to let anglers past. Bivvies were not allowed at the water. Normally, with a prevailing westerly or south westerly, the swim was perfectly positioned so that you could erect the brolly at the back of the swim and sit or lie facing the lake. A north easterly, however, saw the wind smack in your face, so the only way to get any shelter was erect the brolly at the water's edge, at the side of the rods. To give anglers room to get past, I had to lie less than a yard from the margins.

One particular night, the bedchair feet nearest the water must have settled a little as I slept because, when I awoke with a start to a screaming alarm, I noticed a definite list to one side. As I went to get up, the legs sunk even more, dropping me off the edge to land face down in the lake. As if that was not enough, the momentum of my body pulled the brolly in behind me, and two ribs effectively pinned me down. By the time I had extricated myself, my gear was soaked both by immersion in the lake and by the steady drizzle that was falling, and I was plastered in mud. By some miracle, the carp was still attached, and I went on to land a pretty 18 pound mirror.

Very similar was a night at another Midland water, when I was bivvied at the top of quite a steep slope leading down to the swim, where there was a levelled area of gravel. It had been hot and dry for weeks, so that the ground was baked clay, as smooth as glass. One early morning, I had a fast run just as dawn was breaking, and I emerged from the bivvy at top speed, only to find the ground as slippery as an ice rink due to a very heavy dew. I lost my footing, sat down heavily, and then shot down the slope like a torpedo, whereupon I wiped out all three rear rod rests before finding myself sitting in the lake. Once again, the carp was still attached, and I eventually landed a cracking 24lb common!

Just to prove that age and experience are no antidote to cock ups, my most frustrating midnight madness occurred only a few weeks ago. I was fishing a difficult water holding many thirty plus fish, and where runs are hard to come by. I had but one run in the fifty hour session, which came at 2.00am. I was well away on my new JRC extra strong bedchair, one of those that features three sets of legs for extra support. I cannot have locked the centre legs properly, because as I went to leap up, they collapsed flat, leaving the bedchair a V shape, with me inside. Do you think I could get out, could I hell! Whenever I lifted my body, the chair came up to hit me in the back of the head, and if I lifted my legs the bottom came up to trap my thighs. I must have struggled for a good minute, before eventually rolling to the side and tipping myself out.

The mayhem wasn't over yet. Now totally wound up, and with the Optonic still

The 24lb common caught after Tony wiped out all rods by sliding into the lake.

screaming, I went to dash out of the bivvy, only to trip over the low porch of my Apotheosis and once again go sprawling on my hands and knees, before sliding over the wet mud to head butt the back rod rest. There could only be one end to this madness. I missed the bloody run, and that was the only indication I had. Sometimes, I think I'm getting too old for this game!

Naked Ambition
In the late eighties, I was fishing a syndicate water where one bank was accessible from a public footpath that led from the local church to the village. At its nearest point, this footpath came within about thirty yards of the lake. That was the position of one of my favourite swims, a point from where you could see the entire water, and place baits both in the shallows to your right and deeper water plus the island to your left.

I was having a good season from that swim, with several twenties having been netted, and settled down one sultry July evening with very threatening clouds overhead. A good storm was brewing. After a low double early on, everything went quiet and I slipped into the sleeping bag around 11.00pm. It had been raining steadily for an hour and as I lay on the bedchair I could hear the storm becoming fiercer and fiercer.

I was awoken just before dawn by a screaming alarm, and shot out into the torrential rain to strike into a heavy fish. A ten minute slog followed, until I successfully netted a fat common which proved to weigh 23lb 10oz. Needless to say, I was completely drenched by the time the fish had been returned. Sod's law had dictated that the rain had stopped by the time I'd got a fresh bait out.

Because of the forecast, I had taken the precaution of taking a spare set of clothing into the bivvy with me, plus a large towel, and once back inside stripped off completely and started to towel myself dry. I was just about to begin dressing when my other alarm sounded. It was now fully light, and I could see line leaving the spool in a blur. Once again, I shot out of the bivvy to strike into a big carp moving at speed, but this time I was totally starkers. It fought well for a few moments and then I heard a sweet feminine voice behind me.

"Is it a big one," she said, and I turned to see two young women walking away giggling, as they gave their dogs an early morning constitutional. As I glanced down at my nakedness, I realised that the cold water had done me no favours at all!

Eat Your Heart out, Tarzan!
Let me finish on a story from my barbel fishing on the Wensum, near Norwich. One of my favourite swims on the syndicate stretch run by Dave Plummer in the mid eighties was one we called the copse, set in a little knot of dwarf willows. Once inside

the trees, it was a lovely secluded spot. The swim itself featured quite a pronounced depression in mid river, surrounded by streamer in summer. This was August, and the river was clear, the weed lush. The bright sun this particular afternoon made spotting from the bank a little tricky because of light reflection, so I climbed one of the more substantial willows onto a branch about twenty feet up from where I had a birds eye view of the barbel coming and going.

I was utterly enthralled in watching the fish when I suddenly became aware I was not alone. "Sorry to disturb you," a voice said, "but are you Tony Miles? Dave Plummer told me you would be fishing here."

Over the next few minutes we conducted a conversation from our respective positions, until he asked me a question just as I was about to start my descent. Whether that disturbed my concentration or not I don't know, but the next thing I knew I'd lost my footing and pitched headlong from the tree towards the water surface. No more than six feet above the surface, there was quite a substantial branch, stretching almost to midstream, and I grasped this instinctively on my way past, such that my momentum carried me right under it, back up the other side, and then ended with me sitting astride it, facing my companion.

"Well, it saves all that clambering about," I said, trying to keep a serious, straight face, as if I'd meant it all along.

I could tell he was impressed!

Up a tree!

You didn't mean to do that did you?

by Tim Paisley

"You didn't mean to do that, did you?"

I think the average carp angler - whoever that may be - has a vision that carp anglers whose names appear in print are superior beings in some way; that they are infallible, never make mistakes, and catch fish at the drop of a hat. I didn't actually realise that others thought like that - certainly not about myself, anyway! - until an insignificant, but typical, occurrence at Horseshoe Lake a few years back, which is as good a starting point as any to this latter day confessions of a carp fisher type-piece.

Horseshoe is social, and unpredictable. Social is a good news/bad news situation, depending on how you are getting on and who is subjecting you to the socialising. As it happens one of the callers that particular day was Clive Owden, a bailiff dripping attitude and blessed with exceptional good looks. Clive and I have always got on, which is a blessing for both of us, really, because we can both be difficult people to penetrate for those we don't get on with. I always think of Rod Hutchinson as the prototype carp man with attitude. He summed it up in one of the early interviews I put together for Carp Fisher. "I'm one of those 'if I don't want to know you, on your bike' sort of people." Yeh. He's mellowed into a bit of an old softy now, as it happens, but I still look on him through the eyes of an aspiring keenie who twenty five years ago found it difficult to string three words together when addressing him.

I was in one of the snags swims at Horseshoe, the only time I managed to get in either of them. If you are able to get in one of the popular swims at Horseshoe it means that it isn't fishing, but I had to start somewhere and any swim within an easy walk of a car parking area will do for me. Clive was with one of the other bailiffs, which was fine. They parked themselves in the swim for a few minutes while I finished attending to the PVA bag set-up I was lovingly preparing prior to creeping along the margin and dropping it in the vicinity of the infamous wire rope, which was an unsightly but magnetic feature of that corner of the lake at the time.

Bag prepared I stepped down from the swim into the water to paddle down the margin. As I did so I inadvertently lowered the rod tip, and the bag into the water with it. Nice! You are lost for words at the stupidity of such a moment, so I didn't say anything, but slowly climbed back into the swim to start again. Clive summed it up pretty succinctly, I thought.

"You didn't mean to do that, did you?"

I spoke to Clive some time later. After they had left the swim his companion had turned to him and said,

"That was reassuring. I didn't know people you read about in print did things like that!"

Until that moment it hadn't occurred to me that people thought like that. I mean I was brought up on the adventures of Hutchy, who was the ultimate hero-figure, but was always doing things like that, and built a writing career on openly admitting that he did so. Fact is that anglers who fish a great deal and tend to experiment and be adventurous almost certainly make far more mistakes than carp anglers who look on carp fishing as a hobby, don't use PVA, don't attempt to cast far enough to crack off, don't use spods - which bring a whole new dimension of spooling up, cracking off and dismembered limbs into your life - and never attempt to cast within inches of a distant margin bordered by brambles tumbling into the water right above the hot spot. Which reminds me...

I met my dear friend - and later best man when I married Mary - Micky Sly, at a highly inopportune moment on Darenth Tip Lake in the early eighties.

A young and much more sober Micky Sly in his Tip Lake days.

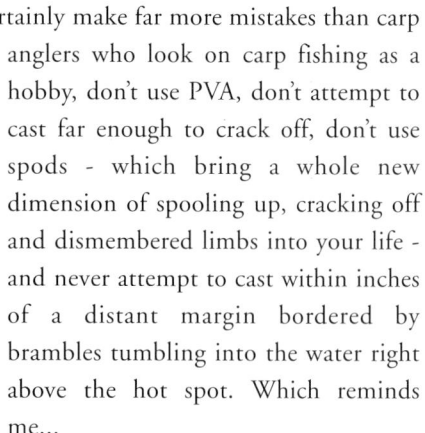

You didn't mean to do that, did you?

26lb+ from the Dry Dock during my first Darenth session in 1983.

Micky was quite a normal human being in those days. He used to call round every day and never once suggested going for a drink. Nor did he fall over, which is a state of affairs which would never exist when he's at Darenth now that it has a bar on site!

It was my first visit to the water, courtesy of an invitation from Bob Morris. I was in the Dry Dock, a swim which was later beloved of the compiler of this book, and was going through the torture peculiar to the first afternoon in a distant swim when you are disoriented, out of your depth, and invariably pushed for time. One of the hot spots that had been pointed out to me was a trailing bramble on the long island to the right, at least 25 yards from the swim. Nowadays you have reel clips and creep up on difficult targets like that. In those days you just cast into the offending snag and took it from there. Which is what I'd just done when Micky walked into the swim to introduce himself. I felt a bit of a prat. 11lb Sylcast was the heavy line of the time, so that was what I'd got on. And the end tackle was in a bramble 25 yards away, dusk was approaching fast, and this personable young man with a shock of black hair wanted to exchange pleasantries. Either that or he was just having a laugh... As it was the end tackle came out at the first heave, it dropped right under the bramble (where I left it for a couple of days) and Micky and I have been the best of friends ever since.

It's not possible to write about Darenth without including a memory of Micky's great mate through most of the nineties, the late Alan Smith, so here's one.

Bill Cottam and I went down soon after the start of a season, '84 or 85 at a guess. Smithy was fishing Jackson's, and was well pleased with his early season result. Five fish over 25lb in the first few days of the season, as I recall it. There was a cloud on the horizon though. One of Alan's fish had got snagged and he had gone out on an inflated lilo to free it, which was against the rules. Smithy was a bailiff, and one of the head bailiffs for the venue - Joe Streeter? - wasn't too happy about Alan's actions and kept going on about how out of order he was, and how everyone on the complex was complaining about what Alan had done.

Now I've had my fair share of the "everyone's saying" syndrome. In the early days of the Society, Chairman Bob Davies used to trot it out, and it meant that

Derek Stritton was saying it! With the passing of time it has become different people in different places, but almost invariably "everyone's saying" means that one person who doesn't like you is having a go, and I've learnt to let it bounce off me. It bothered Alan though and he kept having it thrown at him on a daily basis. In the end I gave him some advice.

"Go to Joe, tell him you realise you were well out of order, and tell him you are going to go round the complex and apologise to all the other anglers on site personally to set the record straight."

The late Alan Smith, brilliant company and a super carp angler.

Alan had a think about this, liked it, went and told Joe what he was going to do. He was hurriedly told there was no need for that, and he never heard another word about it!

He was a lovely man, Smithy, and one of the most accomplished of carp anglers. Cancer caught up with him a couple of years back and his mate Micky could only watch helplessly as he wasted away and died. I often think of him, and his talent, his great sense of humour, and his absolute obsession with carp fishing. A memorable man, very sadly missed.

Orchid Lake could be a disaster area; weed, wind, marker floats and lookers-on being the recipe for disaster there!

Orchid is unusual. At most waters I have fished anyone wanting to find out what you are doing does so from a discreet distance, usually through binoculars from inside the bivvy, or from behind a tree. During the period I fished Orchid there was no sign of any such subtlety being practised! The tendency was for onlookers to congregate on the elevated roadway behind the swim so they could get a clear view of what you were doing. To start with this was disconcerting and I found other things to do, like have three or four cups of coffee before getting stuck into the angling side of things. The problem was that these onlookers were usually waiting for a swim they were going to occupy to come free, so I could either wait till dark, which meant not fishing that night, or I could pretend they weren't there and get on with life. As time went on I came to realise that as far as they were concerned I was just a way of filling in a few hours till their target swim became available. At first I thought they might move on after the first couple of spodfuls had hit the target, but no, they hung around to count the spods, or wait for disaster to befall, or for their swim to be vacated.

Positioning two end tackles tight to a marker in a hole in the weed at distance in excess of a hundred yards in a cross wind has its problems. You soon learn that it makes sense to apply the bait and position both end tackles on the downwind side of the marker. Orchid is very weedy, and not only have you got the line coming up to the marker, but you've also got the line running from the rod tip and through and over weed to the lead below the marker. So a cast on the windward side of the marker is fraught with potential disaster. You have to finger the line down, or cast clipped, so that the line pulls tight well clear of the marker. If you have to reel in for a recast there is the danger that the bow in the line will pull the lead back in an arc, with the chance that it will pick up the marker float line on the way in.

Father and son were waiting for a swim some distance down to my left, and son was whiling away the afternoon watching me spodding - which I completed successfully, without mishap, and quite impressively, I thought. Time to get the end tackles in position. Topside of the marker first. Whack. I lost sight of the end tackle in the air, but managed to pick up the splash. Beyond the marker, but worryingly close to the marker line. I was right to fear the worst. Nervously start to reel in, and the inevitable happens, the marker float ducks down. The weed always turns out to be thicker than you expected, so reeling the two end tackles in becomes a wearisome chore of reeling one in for ten yards, putting that rod down, then reeling the other one in for ten yards - and so on. At some stage in this embarrassing performance the young lad helpfully remarks,

"Your other rod tip is bouncing around. Do you think you've got a fish on?"

To my eternal credit I remained polite throughout.

Fortunately there was no one there to witness the occasion when I was casting the marker float out from the flooded Drum Swim and actually fishing from the Island Dugout, thirty yards to the left. This sounds complicated, but I was fishing the area in front of the Drum Swim, which was flooded, and therefore not habitable. Between the swims the bank is steep and covered in impenetrable bushes, so movement between the two swims is along the roadway at the top of the bank. Obviously when you are fishing like that both end tackles have to be to the left of the marker float. In the big cross wind the right hand end tackle had to be cast very close to the marker for me to get both end tackles in the target area. A couple of casts blown too far left had me over-adjusting, with the inevitable result that an almost cast finished to the right of the marker... Oh no! I've got an end tackle across the marker float line, which is across weed, and which is running back to the swim thirty yards or so to my right. Messy. The only redeeming feature was that it was good exercise trudging between the swims to retrieve the locked, weeded end tackles a few yards at a time. Fortunately the hour long undignified, inept performance didn't have any amused witnesses giving a running commentary

There was a consolation to that performance. Two nights later I caught a mirror carp of 35lb 8oz, from the target area out in the weed bed in front of the Drum Swim.

I have to add that the torture of trying to get end tackles in position in relation to a marker float was not peculiar to me. During one session I watched a young angler go through the full performance of positioning the market float, spodding, positioning three rods (winter season rules), then starting to reel in the marker. That took longer than he expected because he reeled the three end tackles in with it.

You have to learn to be a very accurate caster in those circumstances!

The boys will talk about this one for ever, so I'll tell it myself before someone else does! I'm not really a drinker, but when I get together with Micky Sly I can be influenced into having a social drink - for relaxation purposes, of course. With Micky around a drink invariably tends to become a good drink and I don't know why it is but when I am fishing Chalet Lake in eastern France I tend to be at my most relaxed.

The chalet at Chalet Lake is actually a lodge. It is an afternoon refuge during the scorching hot central European weather that you may or may not be blessed with during your week's stay at the venue, and which we have enjoyed on our trips there. So we adjourned to the lodge this particular afternoon to dine and escape the searing

The lodge at Chalet Lake, a natural social centre during the heat of the eastern France afternoons.

afternoon heat - and maybe have a couple of beers - and there was a bottle of Rickards standing on the table. I'm a brandy drinker, and Micky drinks anything that makes him inebriated. Alan was with us, but his better drinking days were behind him and he tended to drink beer simply to quench his thirst - which sounds like a pretty sad reason for drinking to me. Anyway Micky and I aren't Rickards drinkers, so we weren't going to drink this bottle of the stuff that was standing on the table.

So of course we did.

The afternoon droned on and as the sun swung round towards the back of the chalet we adjourned to the now shady veranda. "We" included Mary, who tends to stay sensible when there are catering arrangements to fulfil. Not always, but often. We were due to have a barbecue that afternoon.

A maturing Micky Sly as we all know him now!

I woke up on my bedchair at ten o'clock. It was dark and my rods weren't fishing. What! Whatever the cause there is a limit to how much relaxing I do! I got up, cast out the four rods, sticked some baits out, and went back to bed, wondering what had happened that afternoon. There was no after-taste of a barbecue in my mouth. I had no memory of returning to the swim, either under my own steam or otherwise. I couldn't think that either of the guys would have carried me back, but stranger things have happened.

Turns out that as the afternoon slipped by and the contents of the Rickards bottle dwindled away my demeanour hadn't changed (I'm actually a good drinker) but my behaviour had become increasingly bizarre. I started throwing things off the veranda into the lake. Micky Sly had apparently kept insisting on going into the lake to return them, so presumably this had fuelled my playfulness. "Things" included the wine bottle, the mustard jar, Mary's book... Eventually I had suggested to Mary that she should take her clothes off so I could throw her into the lake! She had firmly but gracefully declined.

"What happened about the barbecue?"

"You ate it."

"How did I get back to my swim." Which was about quarter of a mile away.

"You walked back, perfectly steadily."

I've steered clear of Rickards since that afternoon. It obviously causes amnesia.

They say every picture tells a story, but the one on the front of Crafty Carper 45 doesn't even start to, so I'll do it. Fact is the lead up to the fish, and the shot, was symptomatic of the syndrome of the end result concealing the circumstances surrounding the capture. I'll begin near the beginning...

Micky, Alan and I went to the Champagne syndicate water for a week's fishing. To give me a break from the arduous haul down to Dover, then on through France, we sailed from Hull to Zeebrugge. While waiting for the guys to arrive for the onward journey I coupled the car up to the trailer. It was raining, and the trailer was parked tight to one of the walls of the drive, which meant climbing over the tow bar frame to get out. This is not a difficult operation, but I somehow contrived to lose my balance and gashed my shin open on one of the metal tow bar supports. It hurt. Not just "Ooh, that hurt!" hurt, but really hurt, like " I might have broken that!" hurt. Closer inspection revealed blood pouring down my shin, but I had to go to Nutrabaits to pick up the bait for the trip so I gritted my teeth and heroically drove myself to the Rotherham bait company's premises.

I must have mentioned in passing that I'd just broken my leg because Richard Skidmore inspected it, and suggested that it needed dressing. First Aid kit out, injury dressed, bleeding staunched, bait collected, and I was on my way. Mary was in when I got back, and the boys arrived shortly after. I may just have mentioned to them in passing that I was in agony, and of course my plight attracted a great deal of sympathy (meaning it didn't). Normally Mary would have been very disturbed by the injury but she tends to gang up on me when she gets moral support, so the collective advice was to stop being a wimp and to get on with life. I was just able to walk to the car so I accepted the advice and heroically struggled on.

The ferry was due into Zeebrugge at 8.00 a.m. In fact it limped across the North Sea on one engine and arrived at 2.00 p.m. Immaterial really, but I knew how it felt, and it complicated things no end when we arrived in Belgium, what with a five hour drive to the lake to follow, me being in agony, and it taking me for ever to set up in ideal circumstances in daylight, and for ever and a day in the dark, when it's raining. And I'm in agony from my badly gashed leg.

Anyway we fished, and a very pleasant week's fishing it was. Or would have been if it hadn't been for my worsening injury, and the three days of unseasonally hot weather we had in the middle of the week. Don't get me wrong, for the end of March early April the temperatures in the 80s were more than welcome, but the first sun blast of the year always burns me, and the combination of a south facing swim, no leaves on the trees, and my macho stupidity resulted in some serious sunburn. Three days of it in fact.

Fortunately I found a bottle of After-Sun in my portable medicine chest, and smothered myself in it. It relieved the pain of the sunburn, but I'd forgotten I suffer side-effects from that particular After-Sun. I swell up, my eyes go all puffy, and as my skin had achieved the consistency of an Armadillo's the relief the soothing cream could achieve was marginal anyway.

I could go on about the insomnia I suffered that week because I couldn't get comfortable with my multiple injuries and complaints but I don't want the reader to get the impression I'm a whinger, so we'll keep the growing exhaustion through sleeplessness out of the equation...

Angling-wise I had assumed the duties of pest control officer for the week. Apologies for the expression but it is one in popular use at Horseshoe when the shoal of doubles descends on you. Micky Sly far to my right had a 30lb common. Simon Horton 100 yards to my left had stunning mirrors of 46lb and 36lb. I caught a dozen doubles and twenties. Consistent action and pleasant fishing, but I felt that my heroism in suffering the twin attack of a gashed, broken leg, chronic sunburn and a distressing After-Sun allergy deserved a big fish. Instead I broke the low weight record for the syndicate water three days in succession.

Mid week major league big fish man Phillippe Cottenier from Belgium came to fish the water. A very nice man who tactfully refrained from commenting on my severe limp and swollen head and eyes. It was a pleasure to meet him but I couldn't help feeling there was an inevitably about him catching something huge from the water to emphasise the inadequacy of the fish I was catching - although in truth I was delighted to be catching them because it meant I was going to take at least a tenner each off Sly and Atkins. We have a tenner on most fish and biggest fish on our trips abroad.

Tuesday morning Si Horton left for home. Phillippe had been at the water sixteen hours and was still sussing it out, undecided where to fish. Half eight the old pan of Spaghetti on the stove trick worked and I had a drop back to the far margin. A drop back was good news because the far margin was fraught with danger, although I'd landed all the fish I'd hooked to that point. This turned out to be a drop back that had snagged itself.

Solid. Switch the spaghetti off; into the boat, remember the landing net (I went out at midnight to land a fish without one at Cassien), wind down to the fish 120 yards away. I don't know why the take was a drop back because the line was running through a mess of an underwater tangle of branches, with the fish swirling in open water five yards off the trees. The tail looked inordinately large. Mmmm. Put the rod down, break some of the snag away, free some line, pick up the rod, take up the slack. The line was trapped behind the spool. Grrrr. Patiently does it Tim.

Free the line from behind the spool. Repeat the snag breaking, line retrieving performance. This time when I went to pick up the rod it had disappeared! I'd dropped it over the side of the boat. Momentary mental panic, then the tip reappeared when I pulled on the snagged line. Retrieve the rod, try to reel in the slack. The line had relocated itself behind the spool again. (I'm not making this up; it's exactly what happened!) The fish was still swirling on top about five yards away, so I guessed it was getting as fed up as I was.

One more heave and the line came clear of the snag. I'd had enough of the line misbehaving, and it was attached to the broken off snag anyway, so I gave up on the old fashioned idea of using a reel and hand-lined down to the area of the fish. It swam past four feet down on a tight line, looking very large. I expected it to drop off, but it didn't. It gracefully completed its part in the drama and allowed itself to be guided into the landing net.

By this time the exploring Phillippe had realised something was amiss and came out in his boat.

"Are you all right?"

I was regaining my composure, shaken, stirred and amused by the incident. Lost for words I pointed to the landing net.

"You have lost a fish?"

"No, it's in there."

He came alongside and peered into the net. The fish looked enormous lying there, with no indication of its depth. I thought it might be the long mirror Simon landed, but it turned out to be smaller than that at 37lb.

"What a beautiful fish. We have no scaley fish like this in Belgium. That is beautiful." Lovely man.

So Atkins did a super job with my camera, and the end result was a series of rather pleasing pictures of yours truly with a long, beautiful front cover mirror of 37lb from the Champagne syndicate water. Fortunately the picture doesn't highlight the incompetence of the netting, the swollen eyes, and the badly gashed leg (which turned nasty and required a course of penicillin when I got back).

Of course I'm skimming the surface here. Things go wrong. You could do without it, but you live with it, overcome, and live for the results and the pictures. A long time ago I realised that in carp fishing you can either hide yourself away, and achieve little or nothing, or you can go out onto the wider stage and accept that somewhere along the line you are going to make a fool of yourself. In the case of the Champagne syndicate water session it was definitely a case of "he who laughs last". I cleaned up on the most fish and the biggest fish bets with Sly and Atkins. I can live through the pain barriers and making a fool of myself for that particular moment of glory!

Every picture tells a story?
Not the complete one!

French connection

by Derek Stritton

In the original "Carp Tales" I regaled you with a tale of body piercing par excellence! The story featured an at the time relatively unknown angler Terry Glebioska, who in the intervening period has gone on to become one of the recent current British record carp holders!

As a consequence, I've had a number of calls from anglers asking me to include them this time, as there may be some kind of connection!

Well, here goes, a range of stories featuring my early experiences of fishing in France some of which I am sure will bring a smile to your face and certainly one of which will share with you another experience of Stritton body-piercing!

I hope no one will be upset by what follows, however some of the early English anglers who visited France did seem rather anxious to share their experiences in print and did rather give the impression that... "French carp were waiting at the port to greet you when you arrived...."

And that every piece of water in France "contained carp of huge proportions, just waiting to be caught."

Gullible fellow that I am, I probably believed them, so it didn't take long for me to persuade the family that France was the place to go whenever we went on holiday. Seems hard to believe now, but in those early days we would travel to France in a Vauxhall Astra car.

Maggie, three young children and me with our clothes for two weeks, sometimes camping gear, and my fishing gear, bait and all were all crammed into one car. However did we do it?

Not sure really, but my first memory of a problem in those days was when the car stalled and died on me as we travelled along the Paris peripherique in the middle of a bank holiday weekend in August when the whole of France was heading south for their holiday.

I think we were in the middle lane!

Have you ever tried to exit a car in such conditions to look under the bonnet?

Well, in France on such occasions forget it!

Each vehicle that came from behind merely shot into the inside or outside lane, in order to swerve around us!

We just sat there with a fearful expression for ages until miraculously the car eventually decided to start again, and we were able to continue our journey.

We still all carry the mental scars today.

I have three other recollections of journeys to and from France, which make me think back and smile.

The first recollection was from the early days, when Maggie and I arrived back at the ferry port of Calais late one October night having driven non-stop from Gien. As soon as we could, we were downing the biggest meal we could find in the restaurant on the ferry.

I think the average crossing time from Dover to Calais is about one and a half hours. Had we realised the crossing that night would be so rough that we would be in the channel for four hours we might have chosen to eat rather more conservatively than we did!

We have forged a few good friendships on our travels, not least of which involved Terry and Rose Thompson.

Could this be another record? Well it worked for the other Terry!

We first met at Boulancourt in the Champagne region. The friendship that we struck led to us sharing a number of French trips at various times. On one occasion we were on a hastily arranged visit to a lake in northern France and we had booked onto an overnight crossing from Portsmouth to Saint Malo.

As usual, we had booked too late to obtain a cabin for the crossing so all we were left with were those dreaded reclining seats.

I think we had all had a few drinks when we tried to grab a few hours sleep, before the dreaded "gong" to tell us we were soon going to be arriving at the port.

Whilst everyone else seemed to settle, I just couldn't, so instead of bothering anyone I decided to return to the bar and a few more duty frees. By the time I did eventually decide to return to my reclining seat another passenger had claimed it.

Make a scene?

Not me!

I just went back to the bar. I returned eventually to crash out on the floor in the vestibule area.

The next thing I heard was the early morning, "We're about to port," message and I was into my second black coffee from the vending machine, when Terry and Rose emerged from the cabin area.

I was just hanging onto one of those round supports. "Bloody hell!"

I heard Terry say to Rose.

"He's still pissed!"

He was dead-right too!

It was sometime before I heard the end of that one I can tell you!

Terry Thompson gets a good 'slap' from a French 20+.

My final tale of travelling involves the Editor of this book. Yes, our Paul, although, I have to say that when I was living the story for real he was well and truly called a few other names than that!

Paul was booked for a week session on Etang de Cailleaux and had invited me to join the trip, following a number of disastrous French trips on my part.

He gave me directions to the lake.

From the peripherique go past Charles de Gaulle airport and take the A11, "It's dead easy," he said.

And indeed it would have been had he not left out the D84, which joined the two roads!

Me, I just went right round the peripherique and was heading back to the ferry port when I stopped at a roadside restpoint to ask a French guy for directions. He took one look at the map, one look at where I was trying to go, raised his hands in the air and said,

"Good luck my friend, you will need it!"

On another visit Maggie, Jenna, Rose, Terry and I were booked to stay in a lakeside house in the region of Gouzon.

The lake turned out to be lousy fishing so we set forth to find what else was available in the area. We tracked down two waters, the first being the local village lake, and the other Etang des Landes, which in those days could be fished by purchasing a ticket from the bar on the banks of the lake.

Terry, Rose, Maggie, Jenna and I bivvied up on the dam wall for our first couple of nights on the venue. The first night was one of those warm still nights following a hot day and as darkness descended the sight of a number of coypu swimming towards us had all the ladies heading for an early night in the bivvies.

Terry and I stood on the dam wall watching the lake and listening to the coypu munching in the reeds until quite late. Eventually Terry decided to sleep, but I was really struggling to settle down. I dragged a chair out of the bivvi into the night and sat watching and listening in the darkness.

At some point I dozed off, being awoken in the early hours by a huge fish crashing out of the water.

The following day I remarked to Terry that it sounded like a horse crashing into the lake! I never quite lived that comment down, especially when a horse then decided to walk into the water next to my swim at the village lake later in the week.

Terry never quite left that one alone, until two years later when we visited Etang de Boulet and a horse decided to go for a swim right where he and Rose were bivvied up. What's the saying?

"Goes around comes around!"

It was during this same holiday that I allowed myself to be "operated on" by those previously mentioned persons.

Maggie and I had arrived a little ahead of Terry and Rose, and I was busy sorting out my rods when Terry arrived.

I was just tying a rig when Terry bounded onto the bank behind me.

"You'll do anything to hide your rigs from me, Stritton," he laughed as he walked by and stopped in the next swim.

In response, I looked at the simple line-aligned and semi-fixed lead in the palm of my hand, and without further ado lobbed the lot towards him.

"Nothing secret about this..... arghh!"

The gasp was about the pain!

The line-aligner had done its business and the hook turned perfectly and embedded itself in the fatty part of the palm of my thumb!

Howl?

What me?

It was said after the event that anyone within a five-mile radius would have heard the profanities as the hook actually buried itself.

Not so!

Trust me, I'm a headteacher after all!

It was meant to hit Terry, but instead the hook went in right up to the shank into my hand!

Everyone agreed that a visit to hospital would be needed!

I had other views, as I wanted to get on with the fishing.

I decided instead that I would use the bulk of my duty free whisky, previously purchased on the ferry as anaesthetic and that Terry would hold me down while Maggie and Rose would remove the hook!

Jenna, she just watched, and reminded me of what a baby I was for the rest of the holiday!

It was on about our fourth visit, that I learned it doesn't pay to be ill in France.

We were camped on a French site with three lakes south west of Paris and our plans included some visits to Euro Disney for the kids and some fishing for yours truly.

On our arrival we quickly realised this was not the most pleasant of sites. We were well outnumbered by French campers and they communicated to us quite quickly that they would have preferred us not to be there.

We made friends with another English family camped nearby, but didn't see too much of them as I was struck down with the dreaded food poisoning fairly soon into the holiday. I was so ill I just lay in the tent for four days getting worse by the moment, leaving Maggie to try and manage three relatively young children who just wanted to be entertained.

Sod the fact that Derek was at death's door!

By the end of the fourth day it was clear I needed to visit a doctor, but as my French is less than good I left Maggie to make my appointment for me.

Derek looks out over a huge French lake at sunset.

Next problem was how was I going to tell the doctor what was wrong?

Maggie is reasonable with French so with her help and English to French dictionary we spent the entire afternoon leading up to my appointment writing my script. Although I have to say there isn't an exact translation for, "when it's not coming out of one end then it's coming out of the other!"

When I eventually got to the doctors and he listened intently to my pigeon-French explanation of what was wrong carefully making notes as he went. Although all I could see was the top of his head as he leaned forwards to make notes, I did note a slight pause when I got to the difficult bit.

At the end of my pained explanation he simply looked up from his notes and paused momentarily before responding in perfect English.

"How long have you had this condition, Mr. Stritton?"

Have you ever wanted to commit murder?

Well I can tell you it did cross my mind at that moment! However the need for medical attention ruled the day.

The final irony occurred two days later as I was recovering slightly and was on my way to the lake.

I bumped into the other English family who asked why they hadn't seen me for a while. I explained about the food poisoning. "Why didn't you tell me?" asked the guy. "I'm a doctor!"

One of the more upmarket places we stayed in France was in a recently converted barn near Limoges.

The place had all mod cons, however the former residents - the mice - did their best to remind us we were only visitors.

They found my boilies and seed-baits and had a field day with them!

War was declared, and I started setting the traps I found in one of the cupboards. Every night after dinner we would sit in the lounge listening to the sound of mouse traps clicking shut all over the barn.

Across the way was another barn with a slightly up-market family staying there. On about the third day the guy decided to speak to me.

"I say old boy, have you got mice?"

I confirmed we had.

The conversation continued. Now please imagine what follows as being spoken in a rather snooty accent.

"Last night they converted our toilet rolls into confetti, and today as I was driving back from the village a little bugger appeared on my car bonnet! I was going so fast that he got pushed against my windscreen so I batted him off with my windscreen wiper! When I looked under the bonnet of my car when we got back just now I found he'd chewed all my plastic cables to make a nest!"

I don't know how I contained my laughter, but by the time I got to recount the tale to Maggie, I was fit to bust!

Last year I enjoyed a very successful session at L'Abbaye Lakes, where I travelled with my friend Rollie and Lee Meldon.

During the weeklong session, I caught a tremendous number of big fish. Never the less the most memorable part of the week was when I was having a social drink with Rollie on the last evening. He was busily rebaiting but needed to borrow my glasses, as he couldn't find his own well-worn fishing specs.

"Sit down," he kept saying to me, so I did, locating his glasses perfectly!

I've been dining out on that one ever since!

All worthwhile. Derek with an Abbey Lake 40 plus mirror.

My final tale is of a recent experience when Maggie and I visited Etang Le Mans in June 2001.

At the start of the second night's fishing on the lake we chose to celebrate the capture of a big mirror and common carp.

Chateauneuf de Pape is a splendid wine and one that is available in quantities in this part of France.

It was the early hours and Maggie was zipping up the mosquito net on the bivvy, when I had a run on the far margin rod.

I eventually landed a pristine 36lb plus mirror, which I decided to sack until dawn. Being slightly paranoid about such situations, I tested the margin depths before leaning on the bankstick supporting the sack. The mud was soft and me a little too far-gone.

I felt inertia leave me as I toppled into the deep margin!

As I scurried out of the lake seemingly minutes later I heard Maggie's distant voice.

"That sounded like a big one," she remarked. "How big do you think it was?"

"About fifteen stone," I feebly replied, as I squelched my way back to find some dry clothes!

Here's to you carp fishers wherever you are!

And remember, enjoy it while you can!

Night fever

by Peter Sharpe

There was once a time when anglers used to practise an activity known as night fishing. "What on earth's the old fool rambling on about," I hear you say. What I'm trying to get across is that strange as it may seem, people actually used to fish throughout the hours of darkness in much the same way as they used to during the day. You're still not with me are you? There are carp waters where the level of activity from some anglers makes your average shop doorway dosser look like an Olympic athlete, in which case the presence of daylight, or rather the lack of it, matters not one iota. Substitute Big Carp for Big Issue, and it would be hard to tell the difference except that Big Issue sellers tend to stand up more often, even if slightly unsteadily, and have better dress sense.

At the risk of this sounding like that old Monty Python sketch, I would like to recount the trials and tribulations endured by the young night angler in the days when double figure carp were a comparative rarity. Bivvies and bite alarms were all home made, and when five-season sleeping bags and bedchairs were non-existent. In fact, if any tackle shop owner had stocked those last two items in those days they would probably have been led away in a straitjacket. We sat out shivering under the stars without even what would be considered the bare minimum of the Arctic survival gear deemed necessary today. In short, we were idiots.

My first night fishing expedition was to a little one acre tench pond, dug into the fen soil at a place which went under the glorious name of Pode Hole. This pond was more or less in the back garden of a farmhouse, between the cabbage patches and an expanse of black fields. To fish it, you just turned up and left your bike in the back yard, then sat in your chosen pitch until the owner, who was called Fang, came round to collect your shilling. I don't think Fang was his real name, but he was a very elderly son of the soil, half-blind, and with impressive hair growths sprouting from his ears. Several times a day he would shuffle around, and sometimes even through the pond in his carpet slippers, thrashing at the undergrowth with his walking stick, and repeating his mantra of "Eyoo paid?" even if it was the fifth time he had asked you that day.

One day during the summer holidays, me and my mate Wiz decided that if we were to fish this pit at night, we couldn't fail to make an incredible haul of the small tench and whatever else might be lurking in the weedy depths. Planning this expedition with military precision, we sat down and compiled a long list of all the things we would need to survive this mission, most of which consisted of food rather than items of tackle. I seem to remember that a single flask of cocoa was all I considered necessary in liquid form to carry me through this long session. When we remembered that everything had to be transported the ten miles on the back of our push-bikes, the list of essentials grew dramatically shorter. These days, I doubt if the wicker basket I used would even hold my bait.

We set up under the trees on the deepest side of the pond, and cast out our brandlings under special heavy floats made from paintbrushes nicked from the school art department, then tightened up our lines and trapped them under pennies, which were balanced on the rims of cocoa tins. We then sat back on either side of the central pole of the shared 42" umbrella, and in the candlelight we would lie to each other about all the things we had done to various girls, pausing only to reel in the occasional six ounce tench. It was impossible to get any proper sleep in this situation, but sometime in the chill of the early hours we would fall into a comatose, zombie like stupor, when the sudden clunk of the penny hitting the bottom of the tin would bring us crashing back to reality with a mixture of bewilderment and terror.

A few years later when I first acquired the carp bug I decided that this method of bite indication was far too primitive, so decided to make my own bite alarm. I had seen the D.I.Y diagrams in the magazines, but these all required technical ability far in excess of mine, which at the time and still is, none. Apart from anything else, how on earth did you get hold of GPO relay contacts and what were they? When I was a child my parents had mistakenly hoped I would turn out to be the re-incarnation of Thomas Edison, and had bought me an electricity set for Christmas containing such useful items as an electro-magnet, an electric shock machine and an electric bell. Using this as a starting point for my bite alarm I looked around for a case to put it in. Many DIY jobs used the ubiquitous tobacco tin, but my bell was far too bulky to fit into one of those, so I decided to make one myself out of odd bits of wood "borrowed" from my dad's shed. If I tell you that the roughly hewn lumps of wood were banged together into something the size of an egg box, you should be able to form a mental picture of this fiendish device. No flashy dovetail joints for me, just nails, which in places protruded through the outer edges in a crown of splinters. The contacts were made from Meccano rods, stuck through two drilled holes, with wires attached between the little nuts on the threaded ends. Power was supplied by a nine volt battery from one of those flashing road side lamps, and being almost as big as the alarm itself, it was forced to trail on the ground, connected by its umbilical chord of twisted wire. As a finishing touch, a brown, bakelite domestic light switch was possibly screwed, although probably nailed to the side for added sophistication. It worked by trapping the line between the two rods, which were tensioned with an elastic band, and a run would result in the line being pulled away, allowing the rods to join together and complete the circuit. Drop back bites hadn't been invented then, so weren't considered to be part of the equation. Even encased in its wooden coffin, the bell was quite incredibly loud, but about half a reel of black masking tape muffled it slightly and made the entire contraption look far more professional.

For its first outing I cycled to Maxey No.1 with one of my school mates, who rather luckily as it turned out, had borrowed his brother's tandem. We set up on the bungalow bank and cast our baits out as close to the island as we could manage with our crap tackle, then sat back to endure a long night. My one enduring memory is of the heavy dew coming down, and of the constant fizzing and sparking as the dew dripped down the contacts. We soon both nodded off due to the effects of the bike ride and the onset of hypothermia, and when I finally wedged my eyes open at first light, the silver paper was up in the butt ring, and the alarm hadn't made so much as a peep. When we came to leave, my bike chain snapped and I was forced to beg the owner of one of the bungalows to let me leave everything in his garage in the hope that my dad would collect it later. On the way back, I probably became the first person ever to fall asleep on the back of a tandem.

One evening I bumped into my mate Graham who was a couple of years older than me, and he let it slip that he was regularly catching several fish in a night from the revered Maxey No.1, whereas I, fishing in the daytime, hardly ever caught a glimpse of a carp, let alone had the opportunity to catch one. After virtually begging to be taken on one of these expeditions, one day he suddenly relented. I think this was because his more usual accomplice, against all the odds, had somehow managed to persuade a girl to join him in a far more attractive nocturnal activity.

We arrived at the pit on the Saturday evening and set up in two adjoining swims facing a narrow channel, rumoured to be a productive ambush point where the carp could be intercepted as they travelled between the two sections of the pit. I felt quite uncomfortable with this tactic, as the water was quite clear, and it was quite obvious that there were no carp anywhere near us. The whole idea of casting a bait out to a fish-less void in the hope that one might sooner or later pass through was a difficult concept for my inexperienced brain to cope with. I had seen a carp move out to the right over the deeper water. Why didn't we just go and set up over there? We set up in our adjacent pitches. Graham had a blue sun lounger an assortment of blankets and a 45" umbrella. I had a striped garden chair, a parka coat and a 42" umbrella. In those days, it never occurred to me that people who fished at night fished any differently to those who fished during the day. I would sit there all night watching my coil of silver paper until I became so cold that I would shake uncontrollably. Sometimes I would get to the stage where I was barely able to speak, and it wasn't until the sun had been up for two hours or more that my teeth stopped chattering. This night was warm and overcast however, and I sat back quite comfortably, cadging fags to help relieve my asthma.

Peter with a good double from Maxey. They could still be caught with antique gear!

Darkness fell, and after a couple of hours the lights went out one by one in the nearby row of bungalows. All indicators had remained completely motionless. Suddenly, Graham told me to reel in and grab my landing net, a loaf of bread, spare hooks and forceps, but on no account was I to take a torch. The dreadful truth was suddenly revealed to me: those multiple catches hadn't come from this pit at all, but from the strictly private one across the road.

In those days there was little street light lighting at this end of the village, and cars were very few and far between. I felt as if I was taking part in some kind of commando raid as we crept quietly past the end bungalow, checked the road, then ran like hell for the hole in the hedge. It was a beautiful dark night with virtually no moonlight, and once through the hole, I strained my eyes to discern a path through the knee high grass which covered the awkward, sloping bank. A warm breeze was blowing into my face and I could hear the water gently lapping the margins, but the rampant vegetation at the water's edge made it difficult to tell where the bank ended and the water began. I will always remember the strange scent in the air, which I can only describe as being a heady blend of wind-washed water weeds combined with a peculiar smell similar to that of fresh laundry. Perhaps it was given off by a unique combination of night scenting wild flowers, but I have never encountered anything quite like it anywhere since. I was tempted to describe it as the smell of ozone which seemed somehow apposite, except for the fact that I have no idea whatsoever what ozone smells like. We tripped and stumbled

An older Peter with a big river carp.

our way to a corner, where there was an area of clean gravel at the water's edge. "Just watch this," Graham said, as he threw a few chunks of crust out onto the rippled water. We waited several minutes, but nothing came. "I don't understand it,", he added, "It was heaving with them last week." We made our way back along our previous route and then decided to split up. Graham carried straight along to the end of the bank in search of another spot he knew of, while I just slowly investigated each visible gap, trying to find a suitable platform to fish from where I had access to the water's edge.

Eventually I came to a large bush, and gingerly edged my way down the slope until I found a place to perch a couple of feet above the water. Although I had been disappointed by the early failure, there was something about that strange scent and the sound of the lapping waves that kept up a level of intense excitement. I just sat there for a couple of minutes, peering into the gloom and drinking in the atmosphere. Just then, I felt sure I heard a brief and very delicate sucking sound. I listened intently. I wasn't sure if I had imagined it at first, or if I had just heard the rippling of the water, but then, there it was again. It was so dark that I couldn't really make out the distance or even the exact direction. Visibly trembling with excitement and anticipation I threw several crusts out over the water. Within seconds, somewhere just yards away yet totally invisible, there was a very loud, repetitive slurping, followed by an almighty swirl. So dark was it beside my bush that I could hardly see my hand in front of my face. Almost by feel alone, I fumbled in my pocket for my tiny pocket knife and cut a nearly matchbox sized cube from the outside of the loaf. I pushed the point of the size 4 Goldstrike in through the outer crust, carefully threading the whole of the hook through, then pulling it back in at a slight angle. I then wound it up to within three feet of the rod tip, dapped it in the water to add casting weight, then cast it out into the breeze with as smooth an action as I could manage.

I guessed it must have travelled about ten yards or so but I couldn't see that far and I hadn't heard it hit the water. I closed the bail arm and carefully took up the slack line until I was satisfied that I could feel a slight resistance. At that moment my heart almost burst out of my mouth as a huge swirl erupted loudly, almost under my feet. One of the crusts I had thrown in earlier had drifted right in to the bank and had been attacked by a fish that must have almost beached itself. My pounding heart was still trying to recover its normal rhythm, when I was diverted by a repetitive gobbling sound further out, followed by a swirl. I felt a brief tightening of the line and a slight tug on the rod tip, but then it went slack again. Another swirl seemed to come from the same place. Guiding the line between my fingers, I gave the reel handle a few slow turns in an attempt to re-establish contact with the bait. The bait, or at least part of it, was still there. Once again out there in the darkness something kissed the surface of the water, then followed it with a hollow sounding slurp. Without preliminaries, the line was wrenched savagely from my fingers and tightened to the reel, which was carelessly set on anti-reverse, almost pulling the rod from my grasp in the process. The clutch refused to give line, but I managed to flick the anti-reverse switch over in time and jam a finger under the rotating spool housing to prevent a disastrous over-run. The fight was fast and very noisy as the fish continually turned and bored away whenever I tried to draw it towards the net. Netting was difficult, as I virtually had to guess when the fish was in the correct position, and I made three attempts before I was eventually successful. And the weight? A mirror carp of probably little more than five pounds, but I felt more excited and elated than at any point in my life. As I slid it back into the water it thrashed its tail angrily and gave me a good soaking. Within seconds the slurping resumed once more. Somewhere far away across the water I heard the sound of a fish being played as Graham was also enjoying success.

I caught quite a few more carp that night, and in all my life I had never felt more alive. The dark undergrowth which at first had seemed so menacing, now seemed positively welcoming as I gradually got to know every nook and cranny. I could swear that I was developing an ability to see in the dark, and was even able to re-tie a hook aided only by the weak, green glow of a beta light. We stayed there too long that night, and when the sun was nearing the horizon I suddenly caught sight of a figure on the far bank, holding an Alsatian on a lead. He seemed to be staring straight at me, but he probably hadn't seen me in my lowly position. Of course, at that very moment a carp decided to take my bait, and I was forced to play it while lying on my back with the rod between my feet. Even as it tore back and forth in front of me, two roach, that looked all of two pounds each, were fighting for the crust that had been spat out by the carp. Luckily he either didn't see me, or had decided that I was too far away to be worth the effort, but we certainly beat a hasty retreat as soon as he was gone,

Well could I now call myself a carp angler? I thought so. These were obviously naïve fish, yet I had coped with the problems of almost total darkness, and I was on a high that lasted all the way through the following week. Although I returned a few more times, the initial excitement and euphoria could never be quite repeated. Success was now expected, and anything less than a big multiple haul was regarded as failure. Sometimes on bright, moonlit nights I caught nothing at all and the novelty soon wore off, yet it is probably true to say that I might never have become a carp angler at all without the confidence boosting thrill of that first illicit night.

This tale may mean nothing to those who have never known a time before commercial carp ponds, but at that time the capture of almost any carp was worth recording, and one of double figures was considered worthy of inclusion in the weeklies. The following winter I caught my first double figure carp from Maxey No.1 when half of the pit was covered in ice. It was just over ten pounds, and was considered so noteworthy that Pete Harvey came over from Peterborough especially to photograph it.

How times have changed.

Essex man

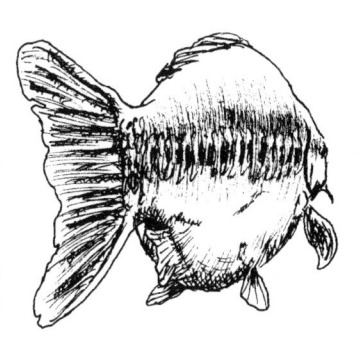

by Chris 'Essex Man' Woodrow

"What I am looking for is a humorous story, or a collection of humorous stories Chris......"
  A lot easier said than done!
  There have been plenty of, how should we describe them.. 'situations' over the many years I've been a carp angler both at home and abroad.
  I've written lots of technical and 'I went and caught this, that and the other' articles for various publications, with maybe an odd spattering of joviality thrown in, but a whole piece that needs to be humorous...
  I've opted for a couple of my escapades, from my very first pioneering effort in France, to more recent adventures in the pursuit of elusive whackers from south east Asia. I'll be honest and tell you that the stories which follow, were definitely not as funny to me then as they are now with hindsight.
  I hope you enjoy reading them, if I manage to make you smile, then I've done the job asked of me!

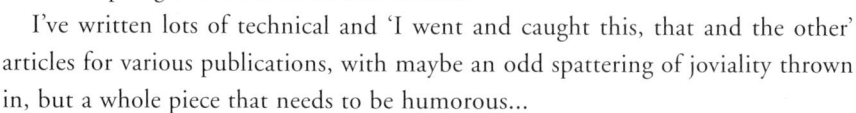

"Trust me, this is just what you are looking for...."
  How vividly I recall those words...
  I'm winding the clock back here many, many years, take a seat and sit comfortably. The Essex Man is about to take you on a journey to deepest southern France with him on his very first trip....
  Picture the scene, gorgeous countryside, great big carp never caught before, headlines in the magazines 'Brace of Fifties', 'Carp Record Shattered.' That's exactly the daydreaming that was going through my mind as I sat in my parents' kitchen, a few days before our planned departure for eight days in France, painstakingly rolling out baits by hand with my fishing buddy Nigel.
  We'd concocted a rather strange (O.K., nasty) smelling soya flour / semolina mix, coloured a light beige colour. My mother had left the house earlier in the day, in disgust I might add, as we'd stunk the whole house out and used every conceivable utensil from the kitchen!

As the rolling gathered pace, and the stories flowed, it became increasingly obvious that the kitchen table was not going to be big enough to lay out all the baits prior to boiling.

My mother's nice clean tea towels on the vinyl kitchen floor were the answer and after many hours of arduous rolling, the floor was absolutely covered in baits awaiting boiling. We decided to have a well-earned break and let the baits harden up a little before boiling. Quite why, thinking about it later, I have no idea!

Anyway, to cut a long story short, whilst Nigel and I were having a sandwich and coke in the lounge, my dad arrived back from work…as he does, straight into the kitchen to make himself a coffee……

I don't need to say any more. I still cannot understand how you don't feel through your shoes something being squashed! Thousands of the poor little fellas were mercilessly crushed, we were well chuffed I can tell you - was this an omen for the forthcoming trip? Could we have stumbled upon a new revolutionary carp bait, 'Disc Boilies'? I think not!

At the time of this trip, I ought to explain, there was very little information available in the UK (that was forthcoming anyway) on waters in France.

Sure we'd heard about Cassien, but the thought of a venue of that size frightened the crap out of us! As we were both used to fishing our local country park water in Essex - of a whopping acre and a half - we were looking for something a similar size in France. Small and quiet, full of big uncaught carp, where we would get no hassle from the local 'Guarde de la Pêche' would be ideal.

I'd made many calls, and through friends of friends of friends, had been put in touch with a rather high profile angler. I'll be honest and say for me, at that time, I was very nervous making the call to this guy!

"Hello sir, this is Chris Woodow, I understand you are expecting a call from me?"

"Hello Chris, have I got the place for you, never fished it but trust me, it's just what you are looking for, stuffed full of big 'uns."

We were both so excited, not only had I made actual contact with a carp angler who regularly featured in the monthlies with some awesome carp, but he had personally given us a secret venue!

How we wound the other lads up at the local tackle shop, gloating on our apparent good fortune and acting as though it was just a mere formality that we would be bagging up big-style on our imminent trip.

Both Nigel and myself were very early on in our working careers at the time and our salaries reflected exactly that.

So, not having very much cash, with a view to avoiding toll costs which we had been told were very pricey, we'd convinced ourselves to take the scenic route and use the 'A' roads from Calais all the way to the south of France, near Grasse and St. Cassien.

This was the second big mistake, after the bait saga, as it took us almost twenty hours! We got horrendously lost, constantly stuck behind every conceivable bloody slow moving French vehicle and ended up spending more on petrol than we would have toll costs!

We arrived in the middle of the night, which wasn't a lot of good, as the directions were...

"On the XYZ Road, you will see the small dam through the trees on the left hand side."

We settled for some kip in the car and awoke a few hours later in daylight to try and find the track to the lake. It was a great looking little lake once we'd found it, reached by a pretty hair-raising dirt track which tried in vain to rip the bottom off my car, which took us all the way to the dam end.

No one fishing, in fact it was eerily quiet, as though totally forgotten about.

Maybe no one else was daft enough to attempt getting down the track?

Adrenalin was pumping through our veins, it was certainly a small pool, but was it really "stuffed full of big 'uns"

This would be plain sailing for sure.

We took a slow walk round, eventually settling on a couple of swims mid-way down the lake where we felt we could cover most water.

Having no echo sounder, we spent ages plumbing and looking for decent areas to put the hookbaits to. Baiting and dropping the hookbaits accurately was done using a blow up plastic lilo, couldn't afford an inflatable boat!

This involved getting soaking wet and basically laying face down paddling with the lead in our mouth and the hook link dangling down our chins. It worked, for a few times.

Then I ended up hooking the front of the lilo, pulling in panic and consequently ripping the plastic, then thrashing about 100 yards out in the middle of the lake.

I was going down like the Titanic.

Nigel was in hysterics on the bank, rolling around like some demented...anyway.....no thanks to his help, I got back to the bank, with the now-defunct lilo.

You're waiting to hear about big whackers now, aren't you?

Well, we worked hard to try and catch something, anything! We spent each day looking for signs of fish, trying different areas, different rigs, anything we could think of.

I even spent an hour one morning digging for worms to use as bait with a bankstick!

After four days and nights on the lake, spirits were very low. Truthfully they were rock bottom.

I couldn't help thinking it was somewhat weird that we hadn't seen so much as a fish roll or top, day or night.

We only had a couple of days left, with no back up venue, no lilo and a load of squashed boilies!

Anyway, that afternoon, we get a vist from a local birdwatcher/walker, who'd noticed our umbrellas.

"Non pêche, non pêche," he exclaimed.

Great this is all we need. Now we're fishing illegally, tackle confiscated, blanked, pissed off, at each others throats, bitten alive by mozzies..... what a great introduction to French carp fishing this would be...

I understood that 'non peche, non peche' meant roughly 'no fishing, no fishing' but, after a couple of years doing French at school, to say I was somewhat disappointed with my grasp of the French language was a big understatement. I couldn't understand another word the guy was trying to tell us!

After the guy had been gone for a few hours, and we'd sat there nervously debating whether to pack up as the local gendarmes were probably on route. However, he returned clutching a handful of photographs. Ahh, how nice, some pictures of the local wildlife, just what we needed...!!

After some rather nice pictures of various tufties and plant life, one of the pictures showed a view looking across the lake towards the small dam. The guy in the picture was pointing and laughing.

Something strange about the picture, something very strange, no water in the lake......several photos on and we sat in stunned silence, we were looking at a totally empty lake.

No apparent deep spots for any fish to remain alive, just mud, odd patches of weed and a trickling of water where the stream obviously ran across the pond towards the dam end.

Totally forgotten about alright! Totally forgotten about because the lake had been drained dry by the local farmer (whose land we were apparently guesting!) some time before our arrival and it seems every living thing had been removed or left for dead!

What the friendly gentlemen had been trying to tell us was, "No fish, no fish!"

We had wasted a whole week. Nigel was so impressed with the top-secret tip I'd received and we'd so enthusiastically followed, the whole return journey was spent in silence!

Talk about having to eat humble pie in the local tackle shop when we got back!

As many of our readers know, Chris did indeed have much more success in France as this proves.

The China Bear

There's a bar in Hong Kong called the China Bear.

When I say Hong Kong, it's actually on one of the small surrounding islands called Lantau at Mui Wo harbour, a short ferry ride from Hong Kong Central.

It was here I met Kevin....

For interest's sake, Lantau has the world's largest outdoor Buddha, in bronze, standing some 79 feet high. 'Lantau' also means 'broken head' in Cantonese by the way.

Oh yes, I'm full of useful information!

Sitting relaxing in the open area in front of The China Bear over lunch with my wife Carol, taking in the scenery and having a few beers, we were approached by a nice fella who'd obviously had plenty of liquid refreshment!

And here is the record sized Buddha.

I should mention that I was working in Hong Kong at the time, and we often spent the weekends visiting the surrounding islands such as Lantau, Lamma and Macau, for some fresh air away from the frantically hectic pace of life in Hong Kong Central.

There are quite a lot of expatriates in Hong Kong, quite why Kevin honed in on us is anyone's guess, I suppose we must look like a friendly couple! Anyway, after a couple of beers, it transpired that Kevin is a keen carp angler - wasn't my wife impressed!

I couldn't believe it, all those thousands of miles from home in the most unlikely place, I had bumped into a fellow UK carp man! It turned out we also had some mutual acquaintances. Kevin seemed to know his stuff, so the beer and carpy tales flowed all afternoon.

Of most interest to me was the fact that Kevin had done a little investigating while he'd been in Hong Kong into some of the big reservoirs. From what was said, he had seen some very large common carp in a reservoir not a million miles from the China Bear and also he had caught a few smaller carp from a pond near the border into mainland China. Better still, he had his carp gear and a few boilies ready and waiting at his apartment. Even better still, my parents were coming out that very week, so a list of essentials to bring out, including good old Tutti Fruttis's were e-mailed to my dad in the UK.

Hong Kong Customs is not that easy to pass through, to say the least, so my parents had rather an awkward time explaining to the customs officials why they had bagfuls of bright orange fish food in their suitcase!

Kevin and I arranged to meet in Central, following the departure of my parents, the next weekend for my first reconnaissance of the water near the Chinese border where Kevin had caught a few small carp from and where he had heard held a few bigger specimens.

'Central' is the main train and ferry terminal for Hong Kong Island and is full of people twenty four times seven! I didn't have to wander through Central for too long looking for Kevin, amongst the businessmen and woman who are rather short, I might add! There he was decked out in camouflage gear, rucksack, chair and rods, ready to go!

We had a lot of gear between us, so it was quite a struggle getting into the station down the escalators, through the turnstiles, and into the train. We were getting some particularly strange looks, especially when we unfolded our chairs on the train, opened our flasks of coffee, and sat chatting for the hour or so journey.

My first impression of the lake was rather disappointing, especially after seeing Kevin's photographs of some of the huge overgrown reservoirs he had looked at.

It was definitely not the picture I had formed in my mind! What lay in front of us was a muddy-looking puddle with rickety timber duck-boards around its entire perimeter - it was half an acre if we were lucky! Still, after all the aggro of getting there we were determined to give it a crack.

And crack I almost did. Well my head anyway, as a crude looking swimfeeder contraption complete with treble whistled by my ear. Now, whether this was a deliberate ploy to warn us off or purely an overcast I do not know. However, as I turned in anger, the culprit bowed politely, grinning. Being the gentlemen that I am, I untangled his rig from the duck-boards and bowed in reply.

We set up as far away as you can on a half acre puddle from our swim-feeding friend, and after a short while had three rods fishing.

Confidence was quite high, I must admit, how far wrong can you go on a pool like this if matey was your average standard of angler?

After an hour or so, things were still quiet, but we'd had a few liners and were poised over the rods ready to start hauling. Another hour passed so we sat back for a doze, I was rudely awoken by not one, not two, but all three rods being dragged sideways towards the water.

No rod rests on these duck-boards fellas!

Kevin and I were on the rods in a flash! Looking across the pond, it appeared matey was into a fish too with his rod held low giving maximum side-strain. Had we all intercepted a late morning feeding spell?

A nasty thought crossed my mind, the gut feeling you get when you know what you've hooked isn't quite as it should be. Surely not? I let the pressure off the rod I was holding and sure enough matey appeared to be gaining line. Kevin had caught on too and was not as polite as he possibly could have been!

The biggest bloody bird's nest was dragged ashore, with matey's damn swim-feeding contraption stuck well amongst it.

Oh yes, we were well pleased.

Matey even had the front to come wandering round, grinning as usual, to offer assistance.

His assistance was soon overtaken by advice, in his best English and our terrible Cantonese. We established that the rigs we were using were apparently of no use here and we should be using trebles with swim-feeders, casting as often as possible.

Further discussion revealed that although he fished the pond regularly, he had only ever foul hooked small fish!

We tried to explain the folly of his ways.

I somehow don't think that this was readily accepted and he would be fishing in an identical manner if I was to return to the pond tomorrow!

I dread to think the problems this character could find himself confronted with on our UK carp waters. Probably a rod rest!

After thanking him for his advice and politely asking him to stay away from us, we re-tackled and were once again poised over the rods in pursuit of a carp, even a very small carp, please. I secretly hoped the bronze Buddha on nearby Lantau Island would blow some luck in our direction....

It turned into a long day, especially as it started to pour with rain and we had no brolly. Thankfully our new friend stayed well away, not so thankfully, so did the carp. Which is hardly surprising, with some lunatic thrashing the water to a pulp thirty yards away!

We packed up, looking like drowned rats, ready for what was sure to be an interesting journey back home on a packed rush-hour train! To add insult to injury and really round the day off nicely, matey drove past us whilst we were traipsing to the train station, grinning and waving!

There are a few more tales from south east Asia, including me snapping one of Kevin's prize carp rods, but we'll save those and our trips to the reservoirs in pursuit of monster commons for another time.

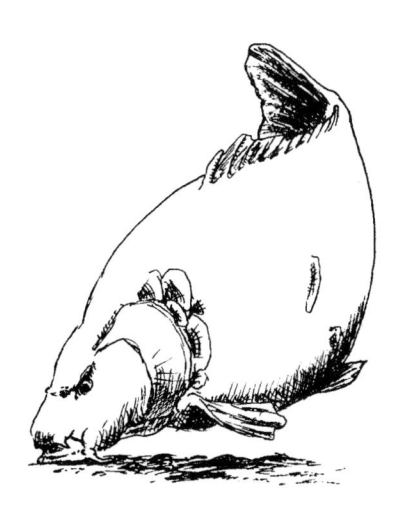

Uninvited guests

by Bob Roberts

Should you happen to travel north, to York, by train, then 7 miles or so beyond of Doncaster you will spot a pond.

It's not a big pond, perhaps only three acres, but you can't mistake it for any other because wooden shelters tower starkly over many of the swims. Reaching high above the pond is the unmistakable shape of a brickyard chimney, for this pond was dug, like many others up and down the country, to produce clay that in turn was fired to make bricks.

Perhaps the shelters are no longer there, I don't know, but it is immaterial to my tale about a time when my driven desire, my intrepid enthusiasm for fishing and adventure was far stronger than the restrictive streak of common sense I was cursed with at birth. It was the day on which the Jonah and I came to a decision that we had ignored the charms of the brickpond for long enough. It was time to pay a little visit.

I must explain before going further, especially for younger readers, that carp have not always been as widespread as they are today. I guess I never even saw a carp in the flesh until I was about 12 years old and that was in the aquarium at Regents Park Zoo. Today it is inconceivable that anyone would make a 320 mile round trip in order to see a carp for the first time but it may serve to illustrate just how rare carp were in those days.

Whether Clarissa was the very first carp I actually ever saw is not certain, for there were others in the same tank. It matters not though, for a seed was sown. One day I would catch a monster like those swimming in front of my eyes.

Later on, a few carp were stocked into Askern Boating Lake and the Willowgarth at Arksey, then Carcroft Pond, but it was there, in a London Zoo, that my first physical contact with a carp took place and you might say my destiny was set. Carp would feature more and more in my life in the fullness of time but on the home front, for the time being, catching a carp was an impossible dream. And those that did exist were of a size that today's jaded breed might describe as 'pasties.'

I'm conscious that some of you will think I'm romancing - carp rare? Come off it, Bob! But I swear it's true. Read George Sharman's excellent book, 'Carp and the Carp Angler' and you'll understand.

Anyway, before going further, I had better make a confession. In my youth I gained a serious kick out of 'guesting' on waters. I spent precious little time on waters that I had a ticket for. Fishing them didn't provide the same adrenaline rush that comes with a fish caught from somewhere you are not supposed to be.

Not that I ever stole fish, did any damage or even left litter behind. I was like the heron, dropping in at dawn, silently stalking my prey and moving on again, long before the rest of the world had awoken. Looking back I was a bit of an angel really. My idea of mischief and adolescent thrill seeking was a million miles removed from the vandalism, violence and criminal activity that passes for 'high spirits' today.

But our life was much simpler back then. We played cricket in the summer and football in the winter. In between times we would look for birds' nests or go fishing as a gang. Hobbies were simple, too. Some kids of my generation collected cigarette cards, others went train spotting. Me? I went guesting, mostly alone, on any water I could find and there were dozens to pick from.

By the time I discovered the pond at Moss I had left school, was working and had transport. The world was my oyster. I'd also met one of my great fishing friends, let's just call him 'the Jonah.'

As for guesting, I'd practically gone straight. It worked like this. If I found a water I wanted to fish I'd offer to buy a ticket. If the owner or club said no, then I took special delight in guesting there. It might have been one trip or a number of trips, that wasn't the point. Honour had to be satisfied.

Anyway, I'm sure you understand by now that I was a hardened criminal with countless other offences to take into consideration should I eventually be caught! It will come as no surprise to you then if I tell you that destiny decreed I would sample the brick pond's delights at some point. It lay on my ever-widening doorstep and sooner or later it just had to be fished. Then came a startling discovery. It contained carp. Good carp too.

One minute I was exchanging pleasantries with a chap, the next he opened the lid on Pandora's Box. He began bragging about a water he fished and the carp it contained. Carp! Bloody hell! Now here was something a little bit tasty. Of course, riff-raff like me would never be able to fish there because it was absolutely private.

Little did he know....

I recall hatching the plan as if it were yesterday. I knew a sure-fire way of getting in there when no-one would be around. I'd fish it in the close season. That way I'd be certain to get the place to myself. Well, I would have done had the Jonah not insisted on tagging along.

We parked up well away from the pond and snuck in undetected on a sultry late May afternoon. We had one rod, a net, a few bits and pieces of tackle in our pockets and a loaf of bread. Butterflies flitted, skylarks twittered and we experienced a few jitters. None more so than when we came across the syndicate hut and crept inside, as you do, for a nose around.

I'd better explain that my 'snout' had let on that a syndicate of bookmakers controlled the fishing and back in those days bookmaking wasn't the domain of glitzy high street chains as it is today. Bookmaking was regarded as a bit shady, the sort of profession that attracted dodgy customers and aquaintances, nudge-nudge.

Whether it was, who knows, but to us the bookies was a den of iniquity frequented by upstanding citizens only on Grand National day. No, they were definitely seedy characters to a man and so the risks, being higher, made the whole adventure that much more exciting. Throw in a few good-sized carp and you can see this was no ordinary guesting session. Oh no!

The hut wasn't at all what we expected for there, inside, was a bed. Perhaps these bookies entertained ladies on the premises? The mind boggled. Rampant fantasies rattled around in our heads but other than a bed, there was little else in the hut.

As we turned to leave we spotted a note pinned to the back of the door. Scribbled in large letters was the message,

WE KNOW WHO YOU ARE
WE WILL CATCH YOU AND WHEN WE DO
WE'LL BREAK YOUR F*****G LEGS

Now this put a new complexion on our adventure. I mean, these guys certainly didn't take too kindly to uninvited guests. Was the prospect of adding another notch on the butt of my rod really worth the risk? Of course it was!

The Jonah was all for finding somewhere else to poach but as I had the car keys I took stock of the situation and came to what I thought was a reasonable conclusion. It was only worth it if the carp were big ones.

We quickly hatched a plan and hid the rod and net so that should we be caught we could feign any knowledge of angling and claim to be birdwatchers. If that didn't work we could run like bloody hell while we still had legs. Isn't it strange how a few simple words have the power to completely focus your mind?

We skirted the pond like two commandos in enemy territory, practically crawling on our bellies and communicating through gestures and soft whistles. And then we saw them. No, not a bunch of heavies wielding baseball bats - in front of us lay a group of carp, slowly cruising in the surface layers.

Out went a couple of pieces of crust and the ripples had hardly settled when up came a pair of lips and the bread simply vanished in a loud "slurp!"

Two more crusts, two pairs of lips and the same vanishing trick was repeated. Oh boy, this was going to be easy. Unfortunately our rod was over the far side.

Then a door slammed with a metallic thud.

"What was that?" said the Jonah.

And then a tractor kicked into life. Whew, panic over, it was the farmer who for some God forsaken reason had chosen that precise moment to plough the field behind us.

One fish each, That was the deal. Two fish and we were off. I didn't fancy hanging around here any longer than I had to.

"Who's going for the rod then?" asked the Jonah.

"We both are," I said, "that way, if anyone comes, we're straight off together."

I guess we were both half hoping someone would show. That way we could sneak away before things got out of hand, or leg even.

Back in the swim the carp were now looking for food. We began to introduce a few morsels of crust and just like all carp do when there is a close season, they wolfed them down.

If I could capture the atmosphere of that moment and put it in bottles I'd be a very rich man. The sweet smell of late spring weeds was intoxicating. It was unseasonably warm, even for May, and dragonflies flitted from stem to stem. Tension was in the air and anticipation weighed on my heart. We couldn't be more than seconds away from the commencement of a battle royale. These are the times when every nerve, ever muscle and every sinew in your body tells you that you are alive and life doesn't get more thrilling.

"SQUAAARK!"

What the f**k! My heart skipped a beat and it was a miracle that I didn't yell out loud. Directly above us, high in the canopy of hawthorn was a magpie's nest and the two occupants were having a right ruck as only noisy magpies do.

We both laughed - nervously.

"C'mon Bob, let's get this over with and get out of here."

Out went two more crusts, up came the lips. Same again.

This time, out went one crust and another with a hook in it. The free offering disappeared, noisily. Round the fish went to begin its inevitable glide towards 'our' crust.

Four yards, three, two....

Blood pounded in my ears, my heart was in my mouth and time all but stood still. The magical moment went on forever, frozen in a still frame.

Quite when the tractor stopped I have no idea. The drone of a Massey Fergusson was the last thing on my mind. Had we not been so engrossed, I'm sure we would have noticed and taken appropriate action. We certainly wouldn't have remained, hidden by rushes, beneath the magpie's nest when the farmer put both barrels of his twelve bore through it.

Quite what the farmer made of two lads leaping ten feet in the air, screaming and running in all directions I've no idea but the two 'guests' were learning a lesson they would never forget.

At times like this your instincts take over. Psychologists call it the fight or flight syndrome. No one in their right mind fights a twelve bore, especially after reading the warning sign. We were off and running like a pair of greyhounds chasing a hare! Bugger the rod, bugger the net and bugger the carp.

We didn't stop until we reached the car and I'll gamble we'd covered a hundred yards before the unfortunate magpies first feathers settled gently on the ground.

To this day I'm pretty certain that the farmer had no inkling of our presence and I doubt he cared either.

Unfortunately, for us, the adventure wasn't over. There was the little matter of my rod, reel and net to consider. It wasn't so much the cost of the bloody things, it was the fact that when I built the rod up from a blank I carefully painted my name on it!

We had no choice but to go back and retrieve it.

Funnily enough, I've done very little guesting since that day.

I can't think why.

Wetting the Baby's Head

Despite our fun and games on the carp lake, the desire to 'guest' on waters didn't completely desert us and another trip remains memorable for very different reasons. Moreover it was a guest session like no other. You see, we were both attending a christening party. No, let's be perfectly accurate here, it was the christening of the Jonah's eldest daughter and I was to be her godfather.

Things went as swimmingly as they generally do on these occasions. Let's face it, the average vicar gets plenty of practise and more or less knows the words off by heart. Anyway, the old vic did the business, we all promised to do what guardians do, holy water was splashed around, the baby cried and we all repaired back to the Jonah's house where drink flowed as freely as you might expect.

I've always regarded christenings as pretty much a women's thing. Babies don't have a clue what's going on, parents do as they are expected to do but female guests get an excuse to dress up in posh frocks. For men it's not quite the same. We blokes tend to wear what we are told to and huddle in corners pretending to show a modicum of interest in proceedings but if truth be told, our minds are generally to be found on other things. A well-trained husband can maintain a pretence of interest for hours, others are not so successful. When I'm pressed into situations like this I generally try to hold a beer glass in one hand, grin inanely and make small talk with a procession of strangers that I have nothing in common with until it is time to go home.

Anyway, by late afternoon my patience was wearing a little thin and I really needed to escape, but how on earth could I? Well, in the books of second rate novelists you will find many instances when eyes meet across crowded rooms. What happened at the christening party was not dissimilar. I'd long passed the point where I lost the will to live and visions of red topped floats kept intruding into my thoughts and refused to go away.

One minute I was in that little twilight zone where nothing else exists but the fantasy of catching a huge fish, or any fish for that matter, the next I drifted back into the real world. Looking up from my near empty glass I caught the same wistful look in the Jonah's eye and I knew exactly what he was thinking.

You probably don't believe in the existence of telepathy or ESP but let me tell you that it does exist and should you be blessed with the ability to transmit and receive you will know that it is a much more reliable service than that offered by British Telecom. Unfortunately the lines are not private and can be intercepted by anyone else who has the gift, like my wife for instance.

She spotted the look that passed between us and didn't need telling what we were thinking.

"You can't!" she hissed, "Don't even think about it."

That was it. Our secret desire was out as surely as a cork exploding from a champagne bottle. I looked at the Jonah, he looked at me, and I swear to you that not a single word passed between us. He just nodded and we rose as one.

"Shhhh! See you later," I whispered to my wife, "No-one will miss us."

And with that the Jonah nipped over the road to a friend's house and cadged some bait. Twenty minutes later we sat, dressed to the nines, by the side of the local association's very private and usually well-guarded stock pond. For company we had several cans of lager plus the remains of a bottle of malt. It was Isle of Dura, if my memory serves me correctly and I can tell you this, whisky never tasted better.

I doubt anyone really missed us and to be honest, neither of us cared too much if they did. We had carved another notch on the rod butt, wrote another entry in the poachers' black book. Neither of us had had the audacity to even attempt to set foot on that water in the past, nor did we ever return.

Looking back, there could not have been a more perfect way for us to wet the baby's head. We simply celebrated the occasion in our own inimitable style.

I'll bet you've been to many christenings in your time but in all honesty, can you recall any of them. I doubt it. This one was a magnificent exception.

I wonder why?

Barbless Hooks Rule OK!
The St Lawrence is indeed a mighty river. There are places where it is fully eight kilometers wide, up to a hundred feet deep and with a flow equal to that of the River Trent. It is also solid with carp.

I had travelled to Messina, a small town in upstate New York, with Chris Ball. We had teamed up to fish against Bernie Haines and Tony Davies-Patrick in an informal tournament. The rules were pretty relaxed and basically, whoever caught the biggest common on a legered bait gained a point. Equally there was a point for the smallest. Further categories spread to mirrors, fish caught on float tactics, from a boat, freelining and so on. The potential point scoring categories were far ranging and in certain cases, somewhat dubious. For instance, prettiest fish? Ugliest fish?

I think you can work out for yourself that this was not to be the most intense competition I had ever fished in but don't let that fool you into thinking that we would take matters lightly. Not when the battle was set to rage over a whole week and the prize at stake, a whole round of drinks!

Day one saw all four of us fishing Eagle Bay, an arm that runs off the main river. To put a scale on matters, the bay runs for perhaps a mile and a quarter and averages about 600 yards wide. The water is shallow and it is not unusual to come across huge shoals of hungry carp in there.

I opened my account with an immaculate 25lb common that fought as hard on the unhooking mat as it did in the water. Unfortunately, my size 4 Penetrator 2 hook somehow managed to push its way right through the fish's lip and out of the other side. Here was one very angry carp on the mat complete with a flying hook. I covered its eyes with a wet sack, as you do, and waited until it calmed down.

Twenty seconds later I had me a nice docile fish. Removing the sack, I thoughtfully placed my right hand above her eye to keep out the light and thus maintain her relaxed state. The next thing I knew she went ballistic, thrashing and twisting like a lunatic. Instinctively I placed my right hand on her face and the other on the wrist of her tail to prevent her from damaging herself. That only seemed to wind her up further. Suddenly I felt a sharp pain in my middle finger. Ouch!

Oops! Bob even managed to get a photo!

I looked down to see the shank of the in-turned Penetrator was flush with my finger, the entire bend being inside me. The fish still wanted to thrash around only now, the 15lb line was threaded through the fish's lip and still attached to the hook that was now firmly embedded in my finger.

Amidst a great deal of wincing and whimpering I managed to cut my hooklink and sort out the fish.

Chris took one look at the hook and suggested it was clearly a hospital job to have it removed. Reluctantly I hopped on board Chris's boat and we sailed up the bay to share my misfortune with Bernie and Tony.

Bernie took one look and then broke the bad news. The terms of his insurance would not allow him to desert his party while he took me to the hospital. If I went, everyone went.

By now my finger was beginning to swell and throb. I could see me being very popular at this rate. Various discussions took place about whether we might just leave it in there until the end of the day. Not a solution that appealed greatly to me, I must add.

Bernie playing a St. Lawrence carp. . . or is it Bob?

Next came suggestions that the hook could be pushed all the way through and out of the other side. Another suggestion that didn't meet with much enthusiasm on my part. Then some wag suggested looping some line around the bend of the hook and giving it a tug while the shank was pressed flat along my finger.

It was gradually dawning on me just how far some anglers are prepared to go just so they can carry on fishing. Then Tony, a trained veterinary surgeon, would you believe, stepped in and suggested he knew how to remove the hook and therefore there would be no reason for me to go to the hospital and everyone would be happy.

I wasn't convinced that I was included in the term 'everyone' but no-one ever said democracy was fair, did they?

"It's only what they would have done at the hospital, Bob," said Tony. "Except they might have used a local anaesthetic."

That really cheered me up, I can tell you.

So, there we were, bobbing up and down in boats, just off the main St Lawrence River, preparing to carry out minor surgery. Whenever something like this used to happen in the old Western films, Doc Halliday used to give the unwitting patient a good slug of whisky. Unfortunately, for safety reasons, Bernie cannot allow alcohol aboard his carp boat. Consequently, this was to be a sobering experience - for me, anyway.

"Give me your hand," said Tony, "And look the other way."

"Pardon?" I thought, but before the word had time to escape my lips, Tony added, "This is going to hurt....."

"Oh shit!"

With no further ado, Tony grasped my hook shank in the jaws of his forceps and, with the skill of an angler who has unhooked thousands of big fish in his time, ripped the hook straight out of my finger.

"Pass the Klinik, Bernie."

"Now the insulating tape."

"And do stop complaining, Bob!"

Sure enough, the hook was out and a luminous yellow band left the world in no doubt as to where my problem had lain.

Funnily enough, I have never so much as considered using a barbed hook on a foreign trip since.

Can't think why.

Bob, Chris, Tony and Bernie. Photographed before it all went so wrong for Bob. . .

Adolf and the Shoulder Monster

by Rob 'Axeman' Fryer

Come on! I hissed to myself, watching with tightened jaw. Just a few more inches... a little nearer. The water humped and boiled as the golden dawn shafts of sunlight strove to pierce the mist rising from the tree-lined pool. The bread crust danced on the gentle swell.

I had waited literally all the hours of darkness for this single moment, kneeling rod in hand, with line curled around my fingers in the dank blackness. This was the one chance I had been waiting for, the one. I just knew I would win this mental battle with nature's own creature and would then be able to walk with head held aloft feeling warm and well. If I failed I would be sent to hell itself to forever walk in shame and purgatory. I suddenly held my breath, as the world stopped turning and the songbirds ceased their morning-glory welcome. All was dead silent and my heart pumped in my ears as the grey ghost-like carp turned silently beyond the pads and aimed for the crust, rising, rising... rising.

"Oi, what y'up t' na young un?"

Whoa! I jumped with a mixture of anger and fear as the blood drained from my head, and turned to see the shadow of Kilimanjaro looming darkly over my poor trembling body.

"Err just doing some stalking," I blurted, as if I had been caught doing something I shouldn't.

"Stalkin' na is it? As tha 'ad owt then?" Man-mountain boomed.

"I was just about to, there was a carp just coming up to my crust just when..."

"Aye well, tha wain't catch owt stalkin' in 'ere lad," he bellowed with absolute authority, "Tha wants ta get a wojum on't'ook, that'll fettle 'em. It allus does."

"A wo, woj...a what?"

"A worm lad, bloody 'ell, dun't tha nos worra wojum is?"

"Oh, I see," I said, "yeah." I did now.

Uncle Adolf was a large beast of a man. He was around sixty at that time, and always had an eternal smouldering roll-up dangling from the roundest, greasiest, most-permanently unshaven face I had ever seen. Dressed in a moth eaten green-brown cardigan with only one button holding it closed across the expanse of a massive, obviously well pampered belly, whereupon the ash would settle in a neat grey pile.

He was the money collector, and was proud of his title and his knowledge of fish in general, and carp in particular. He stood there proudly wearing his black gum boots and dirty green trilby, which must have seen better days, as the band was broken and had been fastened together with a rusty safety pin; espousing the benefits of fishing for carp with a worm.

"Aye lad, I've c'ot many a carp usin' a wojum and they wain't 'ave now't else in't summer, I'll tell thee that fo' n'owt."

I was extremely pleased at his latest piece of immaculate information, as I handed my pocket money over to this big, brassy, scary man. His simplistic innocent aim in life these days was obviously to pass on all his hard earned, lifetime knowledge of carp fishing to all and any angler who would listen, and even those who cared not a jot. I took the crumpled piece of paper, which masqueraded as a receipt for my night's fishing, and thanked him effusively for his advice. He stomped out of my swim with the air of a man who had just been to a particularly delightful confession, billowing a rank cloud of blue smoke behind him. I peered gloomily at the water in front of me. It somehow just looked like any old piece of water, there was no magic there now. The sizzling sheen was now just a grey blank sheet.

I really did have to go home now, as my chances of a fish had been blown out by the simple fact that jack-boot man-mountain had scared any living creature within miles, including my flaming carp. Besides my mam would have been worried had I not returned by 9am. I packed away the small amount of tackle and strapped it on my bike and peddled my way home over the fields. I had been fishing at Willowgarth for two years and I adored the place, but I was not a happy boy that morning. I was pleased with smokin' jack-boot man-mountain's new name though: 'Uncle Adolf' was born in that crazy scorching summer of '76 when I was 13 years old.

I shifted uncomfortably on my bedchair and opened my eyes slowly as the sun beat down onto the lake with vengeance. Where was I? Ah that's it, Selby Three Lakes, home of many large northern carp, twenty-five years on. I looked up and across the water and sighed deeply. I was contented with my lot. I have caught a few decent-sized carp from the lake, but that was not how it had always been. My exciting new adventure onto this large-carp water here at Selby, not but a year ago, had not gone as planned at all, and I had been slowly but surely losing my confidence and ability to keep perspective on the whole sorry situation. I always enjoyed my fishing and of that there is no doubt, but I had traversed a new line somewhere along the way and had steadily lost my grip on the game. A situation I had never ever encountered before in twenty-six years of carping. I lit a cigarette.

I had caught carp before, I knew what I was doing. But did I? Yes I damn well did! Big carp, small carp and medium carp, common carp, mirror carp and leather carp. A green carp, a blue carp and even a carp with a bloody dickie-bow and a bowler hat who told me to hurry up with the un-hooking as he was going to a convention about how to avoid being hooked; how he was the chief speaker and it would not look good on his resumé! Yes! I would, therefore, definitely catch a good-large carp from this water and yet, the Shoulder Monster had not kept quiet, and I started cracking not too far into the year.

"Ah, so you think you know all about carp fishing do you? Hmmmn...well, let me tell you something," it cooed gently into my ear.

"You are not going to catch on this session my boy, hmmn. No, no, no, so you may as well run along home now, and stop worrying your little head about it," it cajoled. "Believe me, believe me, a big pink monkey sat in a tree, all the others are just better than you and you are out of your depth sonny."

"Am I?" I would inwardly ask.

"Could this possibly be true?"

For God's sake, was I going insane? I had begun to wonder about this very prospect whilst struggling at these lakes and all I needed was this cruel voice taunting me whenever I was going through a bad time whilst at the water. I thought I might end up in an asylum full of carp anglers who had lost their way and would be eternally at the mercy of hundreds of mocking Shoulder Monsters.

"You will."

"Shut UP!"

It was June 2000 when a friend and myself started our fishing at Selby. We had booked a week session with the fishery manager Gordon Fowler, and as the ever-helpful host, he advised us to the location of various features and swims and all the rules too. We had always been confident in our ventures to new waters and this was no different, we were excited at the potentially simple prospect of catching a number of large fish to fulfil our own desires as master anglers. As we had been away from the carp scene for a few years, with only around half a dozen sessions per year, we decided to ease ourselves back in with this week, and to learn and get up to speed with developments at a leisurely pace.

The week went well and during the days, Gordon filled us in with more details and showed us the large album full of pictures of large carp being held by anglers with even larger smiles. We drooled at the prospect of impending fat carp and I sat in the bivvy practicing a really wide cheesy grin. Which funnily enough always feels cheesier than it actually appears on film, weird, eh? We enjoyed a barbecue or two and had a great week with a few drinks and many laughs too. I came away from that enjoyable week with a 22lb 8oz mirror and two lost fish. My mate blanked but was not really too concerned as it was a cobweb brushing week.

It turned out after a couple of weekends that he was not able to fish for a while and I was left with fishing the lake alone.

I lay back down on the bedchair, exhaling the smoke slowly through my nose.

And yet again my mind drifted back to that hot summer of '76. Ah yes, those fun, hot lazy days, trouble was there was too much sun! I have always had an allergy to the sunshine and when I was younger it was even more acute than now. It was with this knowledge firmly implanted in the back of everyone's mind that I took myself off to the pool again on the Friday after school, cycling viciously down the lane, past the power station and across the wind-swept fields.

I arrived in a state of sweating frenzied excitement and disarray. I dismounted in a heap and chained my old bike to the rickety wooden fence. I peered over to see if my favourite area was free, it was, and untangled the tackle from the bike. Uncle

Adolf was in the hut. I could see the enormous plume of smoke wafting effortlessly through the sliding window. I cringed a little at the thought of walking past and having to put up with another lesson on how to catch carp. Perhaps I would be lucky this time and get a seminar on human hygiene or cardigan darning, but somehow I doubted it. I straggled forward, head down, hoping he would not notice me as perhaps he may decide to have a brew and turn his back at the crucial moment of passing. I especially didn't want another long prolonged episode of ridicule, which I had endured the last time I was here following my gargantuan battle with a mirror carp from the pool facing the hut. Oh dear, oh dear.

That was a fine day, I remember, my friend Howard and I had whistled and sang our way to the pool on the bikes.

"Ice cold coke on the back of my throat... singing, hello summer time."

We arrived and set up our simple one rod and float tackle in the swims directly in front of the hut. This was unusual as we normally took off around the other side of the lakes to one of the other pools, which were really all one but with a number of narrow cuts, to creep and crawl and stalk within the undergrowth.

After casting our ball of bread paste into the lake and having a great day catching carp of two and three pounds, I latched into a very heavy fish which took around 15 yards of line from the spool in one headlong dash. This was it, yeah, the big one. I had just recently seen an 18lb common carp one Saturday evening as I was packing away, and it had blown my young mind. The largest carp I had seen by far. With bronze scales, it glistened in the evening sunset, transfixing me with its very beautiful existence, as I had never seen such a thing before. I had gawped with burning cheeks, pounding heart, with eyes and mouth wide open.

So here I was, happily attached to one of those superb beasts whilst my heart thumped like a trip-hammer and threatened to explode my chest into tiny fragments. Howard put down his rod and came to my side to enjoy the ensuing fight.

After ten minutes I was still attached and whatever I did seemed to make no difference to the fish at all, it just ran where it pleased and I expertly gave line where I had to, and took line where I could. I was in full control and was simply playing a big carp to the final defeat. Whereby I would then be congratulated by all the anglers on the half acre pool, of which there were around half a dozen. Simple and wonderful. Howard encouraged me, gave me advice and was as excited as me by this great, intrepid, new experience.

I can honestly say I was 'the man' while I bent the rod to the left and then heaved to the right, with a mastery never quite seen before in the world of carping. Other anglers had begun to take notice and one even put his match rod down and got out his flask and sandwiches.

After another 15 minutes of terrific battling, it started. Uncle Adolf burst fully into life, "What thee got theer young 'un? A bleedin' whale?."

This was followed by a choking noise as his mate who must have been his partner from the local drinking establishment tried to suppress a burst of laughter with his hand. I reddened as Howard turned angrily back to me and said,

"Ignore him Rob, I think he's pissed."

I was now really getting a little concerned. This fish was slowly getting the upper hand and had been on for half an hour now, and I was getting impatient at the lack of progress I was making. I had not seen the carp yet and I dearly wanted to have a glimpse of this wondrous animal and the recent heckle echoing in my ears had not given me any reason to take longer about it.

"Oi, Bonzo, I've gorra graplin' 'ook in't back o't van if tha wents it!" Uncle Adolf's second in command fired out. This was followed by a great guffaw from Adolf as he made no effort at all to hide his glee at this hilarious remark.

"Did he call me Bonzo?" I exclaimed to Howard.

"No mate, I think he said Bozo."

"Oh."

I held onto my rod as I turned quickly to see both bent at the waist and rocking with mirth. Howard sniggered in my ear and I looked sharply at him; he stopped.

Oh my god, this was slowly turning into one major fiasco as I clung on for dear life only to behold the sight of sandwich man putting his flask lid back on and lovingly extracting what looked to be a humongous slab of apple pie. From which he broke off a chunk and handed it across to his mate. The other anglers around the pool started to confer quietly amongst themselves and the odd snort was heard to my absolute embarrassment as I tugged even harder at this wretched thing on the end of my line. Howard suggested giving a sharp jig so as to snap the line as he was obviously caught up in this debacle and wished to save a little face himself. That was nearly the final straw! I was even embarrassing my mate to the point where he wished he was somewhere else!

Suddenly I had a glimmer of hope as the carp seemed to ease on the line and I could feel a definite swing of fortune in my direction. This had now been going on for an hour and I was dearly praying that this would be the final stage.

"Get the net Howie!" I squeaked, "I thinks it's coming in."

Howard got the net ready as I leaned into the heavy weight and sighed with relief as my Shakespeare Alpha glass rod took the strain.

"A baht time young 'un, ah was startin' t' think tha wo gonna 'ave t' swim fo't bugger," Adolf sang out, obviously to the delight of Himmler who roared with appreciation at his master's charmed wit.

I was now suddenly seeing the funny side of it all as I relaxed and began to enjoy this final moment of glory, as the largest carp anyone of these so-called fishermen had ever seen, was about to grace my net. I heaved as Howard leaned out with the net.

Now Howard was my best mate and he always said what he felt; his father was a great Yorkshireman who's motto was, 'Say what tha means, and mean what tha says,' so I was not a little perturbed by his next short whispered utterance.

"Oh shit!"

I looked around at him and followed his shocked gaze toward the now defeated carp. He had seen in the blinking of an eye, what I had not. I was overwhelmed at the sight, which greeted me, and my heart sank and my pulse raced as a cold sweat formed on my brow and my elation pitched into foreboding darkness.

This great beast, which I was about to drag over the net was going to be my demise, as my mind raced for words, which I had not even learned yet. Howard lifted the net on the carp, which on first appearance looked to weigh about two pound.

"Bloody 'ell young 'un, I thought tha'd gorra flamin' great tug on theer! What the 'ell do you call that? Adolf roared with great pleasure across the pool.

Himmler, with great restraint and typical Yorkshire understatement replied, "Aye, tha's reet theer, 'ave 'ad bigger roach me s'en."

I unhooked the fish with great embarrassment amidst much sniggering from the anglers around the pool, as Howard retreated to the sanctuary of his own basket. How could this possibly be? How I wished I could have curled up and died.

Quickly as I could I put the little mirror back and started to pack away my small amount of tackle bearing a shame which was beyond words, and was too much for me to handle. I tried desperately to ignore the muffled tittering from the apple pie brigade.

As we dejectedly tramped past Uncle Adolf and Himmler on the way to our bikes, Adolf, blowing a great shower of ash on his belly, grabbed my shoulder and pulled me closer.

"'Ere lad," he bent and whispered conspiratorially looking around him at the same time, "What did tha catch t'carp on then?"

"A ball of bread," I replied a little fearfully, reeling from the beer fumes at the same time.

"Ah well lad, that's tha problem," he trumpeted victoriously, as he straightened.

"I've told thee before, tha want's a wojum on fo't big 'uns. Na think on."

So here I was now back again, bracing myself for the walk past the hut after that last embarrassing episode. I was keen, and determined too, and nothing would stop me in my quest for my personal Holy Grail.

"Na then lad, I see tha's come back fo' some mower," he grinned as he bawled across the counter without a thought to my fragile ear drums.

I hesitated a moment and managed to resist replying, "No I've come back for a carp!" but instead I said, "Yeah, I've got some wojum's too."

Adolf swelled visibly and appeared excited at that response and I realised I was beginning to get well acquainted with his single minded obsession with the lowly worm.

"Good lad, I just knew tha'd cotton on," he chortled with self-satisfaction.

I hurried on, with a feeling of glowing triumph and unadulterated excitement to my favourite swim, which was the first on the second pool at the small complex. I, of course, had lied about the worms as I was currently experimenting with slices of banana, cubes of cheese and flies which I had swatted on my bedroom window immersed in the only alcohol I could get hold of at the time, methylated spirits. Cheese was the best out of the three and I had yet to catch on the banana and flies. But I did face facts too. Bread was God!

I cast out my one and only rod next to the expanse of lilies which covered about two thirds of the area in front of me. I put the rod on my home made buzzer, which consisted of a plastic box with internal battery with two wires coming out to two individual contacts which I kept apart with the main reel line. It was a whole year after that until I realised that I should have been putting a folded piece of paper over the line and slipping that between them instead! My usual plan of attack was to fish in this fashion until dark and then spend all night stalking with bread crust in the margins wherever I could see or hear the carp clooping and tenting the pads. It was simple and effective and I enjoyed every moment without a second thought for sleep or comfort.

The sky grew slowly redder, the sun dropped and lost its overpowering heat as the breeze retreated in harmony. I was glad of that as I set about preparing for the night's events as these long scorching days were not good for my skin. I just knew I was going to catch as I sat on my ground sheet and watched the beautiful unfolding evening scenario. Not a sound disturbed the twilight.

It was now three 'o clock in the morning as I edged

closer to the water in the mud and reeds. I had landed two fish to around 4lb and was as happy as they come. I had heard Adolf clumping off home at around midnight, farting and belching as he scuffed the loose gravel in the car park with his size twelve gum boots. A few short hours later after another common carp of the same size, the dawn broke with a glorious golden glow throwing forth an instant warmth on my chilled damp form. It was going to be another hot day I could see, but this time I had come prepared for any extreme of weather, as I intended staying the whole Saturday I did not want to be caught out and get horrendously burnt or soaked, as had happened many times before.

At 6am Adolf returned to his throne in the hut and by this time I had returned to my swim and was now resuming my favourite method of free-lining a ball of bread next to the pads. I ate my sandwich spread and marmalade sandwiches and poured a large mug of lukewarm flask tea to refresh myself for the day ahead. I happily laid outstretched on the ground sheet and revelled in that warm glow which comes from having caught a fish, and was particularly pleased that I had landed three!

I felt a sharp pain in my side and opened my sleepy eyes to see the looming bulk of Uncle Adolf leaning over me.

"Tha'll get sodden lad if tha dun't get thee s'en covered up, see thee."

I sat upright and looked around to find the pool being hammered with large drops of black rain which appeared to be getting heavier as I rubbed my eyes. The sky was now dark with impending storm clouds creeping slowly, masking the bright blue and gold backdrop.

"Na get thee coat on lad."

He pronounced it 'cooat.'

I looked at my watch, it was nearly ten 'o clock.

I thanked him whilst I rubbed my poor ribs, which were gently throbbing from the kick from those great black jack-boots of his, and he marched off to collect some day ticket money.

In those days, I never even considered saying anything about these seemingly nasty incidents as to be honest I took them in my stride as it was all I had known and hence it all appeared normal to me. Ah, the naiveté of youth.

I did take his advice though and put on my new two-piece all weather gear, which consisted of a nylon hooded jacket and accompanying trouser bottoms to combat the torrential outburst, which was now slashing across the pool.

I watched the ensuing downpour from the vantage point of the leeward side of an old tree and sat huddled snugly in my lovely new dry two-piece with my hood up. This went on for nearly half an hour, whereby it broke as suddenly as it had arrived and I stretched out again in the glorious warmth.

I drifted off back to sleep again and was awakened by a strange uncomfortable feeling some time later. I was burning and sweating profusely as I shakily stood up shivering and flushing at the same time. I was not at all well. It was now three o' clock and I felt the sudden urge to get home quickly as I felt like I was dying. I was ill, and I knew it, and no carp was going to make a difference to that fact. The sun was cruelly beating down as I scrambled to get my tackle packed away. I hurried along the path past the hut where Adolf was entertaining his drinking partner, Himmler, I expect, with readings from Shakespeare or Keats. Or rather I tried.

"Oi, slow down lad," Adolf hollered, as I shot past the hut, "What's up wi' thee?"

I turned and stumbled slowly back to where he now stood in the doorway. His face, which was a picture of intense anxiety slowly changed into one of immense amusement as he grinned like a large Cheshire cat. Himmlers beaming moon face loomed and hovered excitedly over his shoulder in anticipation.

"What th' 'ell 'ave tha' bin up te lad? Tha' fisog's redder 'n a baboon's arse 'ole!"

"I fell asleep in the sun," I gasped, "I was a little tired and I…"

The sudden deafening sound of Adolf and Himmler bursting into outrageous fits of hysterics interrupted me, as I stood there quivering like a rabid heifer.

Somehow Adolf managed to contain himself enough to snigger; "What 'as tha' gorron lad?"

He grabbed the hood and yanked it down to reveal my flushed, red and burned sweating face. "'Ere, look at this, it's all made o' rubber like," he said in wonderment as he showed Himmler the lining of my new suit. "Nay bloody wonder tha's all red and 'ot like lad, ah think tha's bin roastin' thee s'en like 'ot 'taty in that gear o' yorn."

Himmler could no longer restrain himself and guffawed again into Adolf's ear, as I staggered away to get on my bike. With typical eloquence I had begun to expect, Himmler volleyed, "Aye he looks like an over-used rubber Johnny!"

I rode home with just a little less dignity than when I had arrived. When I got home and my mam opened the door, I considered falling headlong into the house as it seemed the correct thing to do. I avoided that and just had a double portion of cheese and beans for tea. And then slept for 24 hours with sunstroke!

So here I was now, fishing the top northern carp fishery recalling to myself, what had been a mind bending personal nightmare this past year, following our first weeks 'holiday.'

The next few weekend sessions I had blanked, but I did feel I was learning so no problem. Hey! It was a new water I accepted that. In July I managed to land a 17lb mirror from the Abbotts Road swim on a homemade dog-food boilie in the dead of night in a torrential downpour, nearly skidding into the water as I vacated the bivvy at warp speed in my socks.

That capture sated the thirst for a short while, but after a great number of weekend blanks I sulked and pondered the gloomy situation. I had met new anglers and I congratulated many on their captures over the weeks and smiled for them at photograph time. The next large carp would be mine I thought, and smiled even more.

Shoulder Monster said, "Hello."

September was just around the corner and I looked forward to this special time of year for the generally crisper weather, although I do prefer October for better catches.

At the height of my desperation in the summer I returned home one time in a state of near apoplexy at the session I had just endured. Nearly everyone on the lake had caught something and the fishing was particularly good as angler after flamin' angler waltzed around the lake congratulating each other on their carp.

It had been so good that this body of grinning merry men were beginning to subconsciously form a society of carp-catchers. Initiation into the group simply consisted of lobbing any old bait on any old rig somewhere vaguely in the direction of the water and an hour later exclaiming, "Fish-on!"

Large leering faces had beamed around the bivvy door, where I was hiding, just waiting for me to say, "Well done" or "Wow, five fish in a session, I'm so happy!" Which of course I did, but I will say this; it's a bloody good job no-one tried their luck whilst I was in the middle of baiting-up or they may have found themselves in the local infirmary having to explain how they had managed to acquire a boilie needle in each retina and a power spike in the rectum!

A new twist on. "Ahh, Grasshopper."

Not to mention the endless flexible bodily opportunities for inserting a simple nut-drill!

Shoulder Monster emerged again and started to whisper deadly proclamations in my sleep, and infiltrated my dreams whilst awake over the next few weeks, at home and at the lakes.

"Do you realise yet that you're making a fool of yourself every time you go fishing?" It would smoulder into my ear, "Even that fellow who turned up all pink and smelling of expensive perfumes on his first carp fishing expedition managed to land a twenty seven from the only swim that was left."

He slimed, "You remember Axeman (Ha!) the guy who you advised to get some practice in on an easy water before he tackled a lake like this. You know Axe, the crew-cut chappie with the air of innocent naiveté. Not you, you Olde Boy!"

I vigorously shook my shoulders at these declarations of incompetence and beat away the relentless Monster's ... truth?

September flew by without so much as a single consolation bleep from the buzzers for my efforts. I had changed my lines and rigs and also my bait, which by this time had taken the form of a number of different purchases of proprietary company baits at the expense of what already had become a meagre personal existence at home. I was nearly defeated and severely mentally exhausted; yet held onto a glimmer of hope borne out of previous experience over my years in carp fishing. It was no joke as I continued to struggle for a fish from the lakes leading into November, whereby I had to hang up my rods because I could no longer afford to fish. My commission-based job was declining and I had no way of providing the means.

Shoulder Monster murmured incomprehensible solicitations over the winter months and through the Christmas period, until March whereupon I drew new strength from the filtered warmth of the fresh spring sunshine.

I ventured forth and spent a frozen weekend in the Point Swim, whereby on the Friday night a couple of lads I had just met saw me trying frantically to defrost some frozen spare ribs in a frying pan in the freezing gale force winds, outside my ancient overwrap. In the dark. Luckily my eternally futile plight was recognised and they asked me if I wanted to get warmed up and have a share of their Chinese meal, which through blue lips and petrified epiglottis I accepted. I yet again had to accept on this occasion that I was not destined to catch my big carp from this water. But I will admit, after half a chicken fried rice, special curry and a mixture of brandy and whiskey in vast quantities in a warm bivvy, that particular night, frankly my dears, I really did not give a damn.

To cap off that particular session I returned home to be greeted by a neighbour's young son as I was falling out of the car.

"You bin fishin' then?" he enquired.

"Yes, carp fishing, just the weekend."

"Catch owt?"

"No son, not this time..."

"What! You've been fishing for two days and you never caught owt?"

It was an accusation rather than a question.

"No, carp fishing is like that sometimes, in fact it's all about waiting ..." and before I could stop myself I went on to admit, "...it's been a while since I had a fish actually." I suddenly grimaced inwardly at this foolish revelation.

"When was that then?" he persisted with sudden wide eyed interest at the possibilities of a good story.

"Err July last year... you see carp fishing is all about..." I trailed off.

The young lad walked away shaking his head without even giving me the benefit of a simple disgusted grunt. He had his story already and obviously couldn't wait to pass it on! He told his sister it appears as a few days later I received a small parcel on the doormat containing a key-ring with a plastic fish on it, with a note:

"Dear Rob, my brother asked me to buy this for 'that bloke who never catches 'owt.'"

Damn cheek! Apart from a suggestion from my father to start using annatto in my bait, this was getting simply and utterly preposterous!

Shoulder Monster peered at the note and slowly turned his ugly head toward me and smiled. That was the only time it found no need for words.

This was the period I also acquired the contract with Gordon and Paul at Selby to design and host the Three Lakes website. To which, I would be adding weekly catch reports amongst other news. I needed the distraction. Or did I?

April arrived after March, which was funny as I thought it was a leap year. My weekend session at the lakes produced a run! A small mirror of around 8lb smiled up at me, and all I could do was look skywards and thank the carp-gods for this small but pretty mercy, on April the 1st.

Hosting the website did indeed have a bearing on my personal mental state as Gordon phones the weekly catch reports through, and I input the data and upload the new page. No problem, apart from the fact that after a few weeks I found this started getting to me considering my appalling and continuing poor show at the lakes. Whereby I will add, I had acquired a new nick-name of 'Blankman' from one or two other regulars. Only the frightfully witty ones of course. I knew this title would be shaken off eventually, but for now what could I do? So I laughed along with the jokes, digging deep for the faith I knew lay there, waiting to come to fruition. And to add more woe to this situation, Gordon insisted on venting his personal venomous dislike of my 20 year old overwrap by suggesting that a lighted gallon of petrol would do it no harm. He then added a few words to this by saying that he thought I was the unluckiest angler he has ever met. I was really pleased at these statements. I always did believe in catharsis, and took great heart in the fact that he probably felt better after that.

The weekly catch reports for the website read like a list of who's who: eighteen twenties and one thirty. Twenty twenties and two thirty's. Sixteen twenties two thirties and a great white. Twenty three twenties, three thirties, four great white's and a killer whale! Twelve high twenties, eight thirties, nine great white's, six killer whales

Selby Three Lakes.

and one yet undiscovered species weighing in at three hundred and two pounds! My god! Stop the world, my head wants to get off! I was verging on total insanity every week the reports came in. The same names cropped up along with Mr Newbie who only decided to go carp fishing at the last moment as his keep net had sprung a hole the week before, and had managed to extract seven large carp. And he did it between 9am and 5pm! My head was spinning as I took in the sheer outrageous impertinence of it all. Then I had to upload his smiling 'how did I do this?' pictures onto the web. Every picture of an angler thereafter that had those 'Grasshopper eyes' I was beat. However I would not be beaten.

The rest of April and May flew by where I managed to witness the capture of two Selby beauties. I tried to run away, but I was caught by my camera strap. Firstly in the shape of Clarence, which is one of the lakes most sought after sleek immaculate carp at an all time highest weight of 31lb 2oz, followed very closely by the queen herself, Lucy at 33lb and 4oz. I do consider myself lucky to have witnessed both of these superb fish, but I am surprised I managed to take decent photo's considering the volume of water in my eyes.

Oh dear, June appeared out of the blue where I suddenly and with sinking heart, realised that a whole year had passed since I had bounded merrily onto the lake, like

Tigger out of Winnie The Pooh, and privately proclaimed my piscatorial domination. Now I felt like Piglet with a broken ankle. Shoulder Monster pounced on this opportunity to claim its well worn seat and accompany me all the way to Selby for what must have been the twenty fifth time. I shrugged and shrugged, but it had such a grip I could not release those callous claws.

Arriving in the car park at opening time on the Tuesday, I walked around the lake and eventually chose the Dockleaves Swim for my two day stint. I was aware of a weather forecast of a changing wind, which would blow, in a favourable direction through the cut through on my left in an estimated 24 hours. I had limited bait at my disposal and chose the increasingly popular and successful method of using PVA bags. The rigs were short hook lengths of Snakeskin to long shank nailers and I was as keen as ever to make the most of the situation. I cast two rods into the cut and one into a further bay and baited lightly around all three.

The Point Swim, next door, was occupied by Julian Cundiff and I also met another angler called Dave, fishing the Kennel Swim adjacent. Julian returned from work and promptly landed a 20lb mirror at which, yet again, Mr Website Photographer extraordinaire leapt into action to digitally immortalise another Selby capture. We all joked that evening with various carp related tales and yet, again I went to sleep that night wondering what the hell I was doing wrong. I am always

Looking out over the rods.

pleased with somebody else's capture and yet that night was spent in more troubled thought.

The following morning Dave landed a 23lb mirror from his section of the cut, and I again took the photos and congratulated him, and it was well deserved too. It was his personal best carp and he was ecstatic at his capture.

The following day passed pretty uneventfully apart from Dave's buzzer alerting me to another run, which turned out to be a foul-hooked 27lb mirror. I had left my chair like a rocket to the sound of his buzzer and seriously considered a career in photography as my hand grabbed the camera automatically at the sound. I had considered a career in 'chair leaving' but I could not really think how it would benefit me.

Julian returned from work that afternoon and took another carp from the cut next to the point, this time at 21lb. I called him a mullet, and felt a whole lot better.

I awoke suddenly to the sound of nothing, and yet a constant painful bruise on my shoulder reminded me where I was.

I scanned the water in front of me and slowly came to grips with the fact that I would be leaving this morning. I had left one of the baits in the cut for 24 hours now as I was following some early information about the Selby carp being very wary at times, and I saw no harm whatsoever in using this to my hopeful advantage on one of the rods. I looked down at the three rods lined up, and realised my futility at willing one of the indicators to move.

I made Dave a coffee and took it around to his swim, yes unbelievable isn't it? and sat back at my own, preparing myself for the inevitable time when I would be packing up and going home to face the usual concerned questions from my family.

"Not caught anything again son? Never mind. Are you using the correct bait? Don't fish like worms.?"

"Yes they do but!..."

I would give in and realise of course their intentions were proper and right and I would once more succumb to the inevitable cups of tea and offers of cake. In fact one of these times my dear mother tried to overcome my anguish with a large piece of mature cheddar cheese! I scratched my ear with that one!

I was packing the gear away, making sure my brain was in the correct compartment of my rucksack, when Dave's buzzer cried out again. I threw myself into unconscious action and launched myself in the direction of his swim, camera in hand. Hang on, a second old boy, something was surely amiss. The sound of the buzzer did not follow my head, the stereo sound-field directed my head toward my own rods. I looked and with absolute amazement saw my left hand rod bending at an alarming degree toward the cut. The 24 hour rod was awake!

"A duck, matey!"

"Get lost, Shoulder!"

I leaped the whole distance from the top of the bank to the rod and struck. The rod bucked and protested at this personal effrontery. Dave came around and picked up the net to lay in the water and at that moment all went solid. My brain cried out in torment and in that same moment I nearly collapsed at the sheer pressure I then felt. Dave dropped the net and had a look from the cut-through, from which he returned and stoutly made a vow to go in for the fish if necessary. I was just on the verge of giving him a good kick in that watery direction when the fish lunged and all came free. The rod took on a new curve and I nearly re-coloured my underwear at this momentous moment. Dave drew new life from the occasion and started to get excited on my behalf which to be fair was understandable. But I had to be courteous and ask him to be quiet as the fish was not on the bank and I no longer had the power of coherent speech. I could not talk. I could barely breathe!

After about ten minutes of lunging and diving under the rod tip I felt a sudden easing of pressure and I drew the carp over the sunken net. I hollered across the lakes with sheer relief.

We took the carp up onto the bank and Dave congratulated me on the capture. All I could think of saying was "That'll do me!"

After weighing on one set of scales I asked Dave to get another set from 'Plug' who was fishing in the car park as the needle was tipping in and out. I was meanwhile holding back months of frustration and anguish and personal suffering, if it could be so-called. A sweep of many personal emotions passed through me in the time it took for Dave and Steve to return. After removing the sling from the equation we eventually arrived at a conservative opinion of 29lb 8oz. I nearly wept at the mental release of it all. This was no nationally recognised fish. Nor was it on the scale of record proportions and even more important, did not have a name. But as I took a last fleeting glimpse of her sweeping tale as she melted into the depths, I could not remember a single time when I felt a personal carp capture had been so sweet.

I packed away in a dream state and called Gordon to tell him my good news, and asked him to hold off with that gallon of petrol as I would be back. He was really pleased for me as I knew he would be. As I opened the car door to go home I suddenly felt a heavy weight slither from my shoulders.

I knew what it was, and I laughed and rejoiced with deep satisfaction at that fantastic moment too.

Adolf and the Shoulder Monster   119

It all comes right in the end. Rob returning a hard won fish.

Battle of the pikeys

by Dave Lane

It was now late August and I suppose I'd been living on Wraysbury for pretty much most of the summer. As a result of which I'd seen a fair few goings on among the local non-fishing fraternity. The night's events about to unfold before me would knock the rest into a cocked hat.

I'd spent the previous four nights fishing in four different swims. I just couldn't seem to settle anywhere. The fish had stayed elusive throughout and I'd walked right around the pit at least once a day. I'd fished in the most likely-looking swim each night, but I remained fishless for my efforts. This particular day I'd seen a 'maybe' at the mouth of the Dredger Bay, so a move into the right hand swim had seemed like a good idea. It was a good spot to hopefully intercept any fish that might be passing through into the North Lake.

Since my capture of Mary's Mate from here a month previously, my enthusiasm

Dave well happy with Mary's Mate.

had returned for the Dredger Bay. It was, however, to be short-lived. Having totally lost track of days, I didn't realise it was a Friday until I'd already set-up and got my baits out. I usually gave the peninsula swims, of which this was the end one, a miss at the weekends, as the level of nuisance activity from the kids swimming, partying, and generally loitering with intent could be a bit off-putting to say the least.

I'd managed to pull the van out of sight behind the bushes and there were a few other anglers around me. Most of these were in positions more likely to draw any flak, as it were, so I made up my mind to stay put. I was in the right hand deeper swim of the Dredger Bay and recently set-up in the left hand swim, which was separated from me by a small marshy copse of trees, was one of the new members and his girlfriend.

The afternoon had passed quite uneventfully, and most of the time had been spent unsuccessfully trying to scare the living daylights out of the local coot population that always presented such a problem in this swim. With all the far banks being made up of three islands they could hole up quite safely. They would wait for you to lose interest in them just long enough to send out a raiding party, grabbing another half a dozen boilies, before scurrying off for cover from another futile hail of projectiles emanating from my bivvy.

Just on dusk, a crashing in the bushes to my left heralded the arrival of one very flustered-looking Irish youth. In between furtive looks over his shoulder he blurted out, "Oim being chased by some big blokes. Dere troiying to foking kill me dey are!"

This was all I needed! In the distance, I could hear the bellowing of death threats and general abuse.

"Can oi pretend oim fishing wid you?"

I could hear the shouts getting closer and there were obviously more than one or two of them.

"What have you done to upset that lot then?" I asked.

"Oi never did a ting, oi only went out wid his daughter," he said. "Oi was wid me mates but they legged it through the woods."

I couldn't see me convincing a baseball-bat wielding lynch mob that matey was a carp angler. Besides, it was none of my business, so I told him his best bet was to hide somewhere in the woods. I wanted nothing to do with any of it. No sooner had he disappeared, than another much bigger bloke came panting to a halt at the back of my swim. "Have you seen a little fokker with curly hair come past here?"

"I dunno mate," I said trying to be as diplomatic as possible. "I heard someone crashing about in the bushes earlier."

He shot off in hot pursuit. I decided to retire into the bivvy until the whole lot of them had disappeared. After half an hour of hollering and shouting, the chase seemed to drift off to another part of Wraysbury. A few minutes later my neighbouring angler popped round to find out if I had any idea as to what the bloody hell was occurring. According to him, the lynch mob had been at least twenty handed and armed with a various assortment of blunt instruments. As we sat there chatting, I heard a twig snap in the bushes to my right. I knew there were no other anglers down there and the only other swim was the half finished Over the Fence that I'd built myself and I'd have seen anyone arriving. So, taking Fat Sam with me, I set off to investigate. In the back of my mind, I knew what I was going to find before I got there and sure enough there he was, down by the water's edge smoking a fag.

He practically left his skin when he looked up and saw me standing there.

"Oh Jezus. I didn't hear you coming, I thought it was them, you nearly gave me a heart attack."

"They've long gone mate," I said. "Best you skidaddle before they get back," I added, desperately wanting rid of him as soon as possible. After a few minutes, he warily made his way back down the peninsula towards the gate in search of his mates. I followed behind at a distance keeping to the shadows and out of sight until I was sure he was on his way.

By the time I got back to my swim, matey from next door had trotted off back to his rods, so I brewed up a nice cup of tea and, setting up the low chair, settled down to enjoy the eventual peace and quiet of the night. No sooner had I got comfortable, than I heard voices returning and having already had more than enough excitement for one night I picked up my tea and backed into the shadows of the trees from where I could see without being seen. Three people rounded the corner leading into my swim, two of them had torches which they shone at the car and on the back of my bivvy as they approached. I stepped a little further back keeping another confrontation as a final option.

"Hello, is anyone there?" boomed a voice. "This is the police."

I felt a bit of a prat emerging out of the pitch black of the bushes drinking a cup of tea, but I tried to act nonchalantly regardless. There were two coppers and they had the Irish kiddy secured firmly between them. It transpired that the girl that he'd been with earlier and her mate had legged it during the family feud, or something like that, and the law had been called in to find them, as they were only fifteen. Eventually, they left saying that if they'd had no joy by midnight they may have to consider a helicopter search of the area, and if this should happen could I please stay in my vehicle for easy identification.

Now, it was obvious to me, and by the look on his face obvious to the young kiddy, that the two girls had legged it round to a friend's house, too scared to face their dads. They were at this very moment probably concocting matching alibi's and blissfully ignorant of the full scale search being launched on their behalf, but I suppose nowadays you can't be too careful.

So it was that, about one o'clock in the morning, just as I was finally nodding off to sleep, I heard the approaching 'wokker, wokker, wokker' of the police helicopter as it started its search at the base of the peninsula, and within a few minutes using a heat-seeking camera he was hovering noisily above my bivvy. Then came the spotlight. I thought it was going to melt the top of my brolly it was so bright. I climbed back out of bed, resigned to a night of no sleep, and went and sat in the car like a good boy. After a while, my thirst got the better of me and I decided to make a cup of tea. The helicopter was still directly above me which meant for the first time ever I didn't have to search in the dark for the lighter and tea bags. In fact, I was considering putting on some sunblock. Two different coppers arrived and asked me all the same questions as the first two had and, eventually satisfied that I wasn't two teenage girls, they radioed through to the helicopter and away they all went. Any slight chance that may have been left of catching a fish that night soon disappeared, as the chopper did a quick circuit of the bay in front of me, illuminating the bottom with his mega spotlight and whipping up the surface in the down draft from his rotor blades.

By about two thirty in the morning peace descended once more over Wraysbury, so packing away the low chair and locking up the van, I climbed into the sleeping bag intent on salvaging some amount of sleep from this nightmare. But, once again, Mr Reality had other plans for me and before I'd even zipped the bag up I heard the all too familiar sound of footsteps approaching. I tried pretending to be asleep, but it is easier said than done when six feet of copper attached to three feet of sabre-toothed Alsatian is standing in your doorway coughing politely.

Sam, who'd slept on oblivious up until now, suddenly smelt the other dog and flew out from under the bed growling and barking as she came. Luckily, she had the good sense to hold back on the actual attacking part or I'd probably still be picking bits of her out of the trees now. All the same questions were repeated, had I seen? Did I know? Who, what, why? He seemed satisfied with my well rehearsed answers and finally wandered off to quiz someone else. The sky was just beginning to turn a deep blue around the edges as I eventually clambered back to bed. I'd already made up my mind that as soon as I woke up the first thing on the agenda was a relocation.

If this was a typical Friday night on the peninsula I certainly didn't want to know about Saturday.

All the aggro was worth it though. Dave with Mallin's at a very honest 39.15ozs.

Photographic faux pas and camouflage

by Chris Ball

The successes and disasters that befall the carp angler as he goes about the task of outwitting an often-tricky quarry, has been documented tens of thousands of times.

The recent capture of a big fish can dominate thoughts for weeks and months, and, as anglers, we have no trouble regaling either in conversation, or words, the events that took place.

But memories gradually fade as time goes by, other triumphs overtake earlier ones. Things also change in people's lives too; different job, getting married, moving house and so on. This all has an effect on the memory of that special day when a worthwhile catch was made.

But we have a saviour - the camera! Pictures of big fish or certain events jar the memory often bringing back into clear focus the whole marvellous occasion. All this can happen by the simple virtue of looking at a photograph.

Cameras are something which are automatically packed when going fishing these days, indeed some carp anglers have become keen photographers as a result of going fishing in the first place. Because we no longer kill our catch, the level to which we want to preserve that memory has brought about a level of photographic competence in many carp anglers.

Photographic Faux Pas

So far I've only mentioned the positive, like big fish and personal achievement - but life isn't all like that as anyone will testify. This was shown to be the case when a year or two back, I found an old (so old I had black hair!) photograph of a fish I landed back in the summer of 1972.

This picture would still be hidden had it not been for the fact that I went through an old archive file, looking for some fish or other. When I came across this picture it immediately brought a smile to my face. So it is with great delight that I can at last tell the tale.

Dark and mysterious - Waggoners Wells years before I fished it.

Having lived in and around the Guildford area for most of my life, I've been blessed with a multitude of carp waters to fish. Back in the early 1970's, in common with most dedicated carp men, I studied Ordnance Survey maps with relish as the quest continued to find a seemingly unknown lake that may harbour giants. At one time or other it appeared I'd gathered a collection of OS maps, some of which broadened the search into the neighbouring county of Hampshire.

One place that had a history concerning carp in Hampshire was Waggoners Wells. Situated close to the village of Grayshot, not far from the area called the Devils Punchbowl. This huge depression in the ground has on its western side an area of even land, however once you passed through Grayshot village travelling north, at a right hand bend, a small road branches off to the left. Travelling down this lane, straightaway it's obvious that you are going deeper and deeper into the countryside. For some way it leads the visitor headlong down into another valley and anyone might reason that somewhere at the bottom lay some sort of watercourse.

It's important to know that the land around the whole area belongs to the National Trust, Waggoners Wells being treated as a beauty spot, which it certainly is.

During the 1971 season I made a number of journeys to this smallish carp pool, there being a number of other lakes along the same valley, though only one had a colony of carp. I tried all manner of tactics to try and catch one of the elusive WW carp. Worse still was the fact that they were often visible just cruising around, and because of the steep sides, once you climbed 20 yards or so up, you could watch them journeying mid water as well. They occasionally took floating crust, but never mine, the wonder bait of the time, sausage meat, gave little response either. Worms, flake, cheese and bread paste faired little better. I always seemed to come away frustrated and it has to be said, at times, feeling water-licked.

To regain composure the Fox & Pelican public house in the centre of Grayshot gave some relief. It saw me enough times that summer, a forlorn-looking figure sat in a corner pondering on the impossibility of catching carp.

Time went by and the following summer, set with renewed confidence and the season only a few weeks old, I decided on a return visit - my faith being bolstered only a few days before by a carp angler I knew who lived at Epsom - Chris Yates.

At this time Chris had elevated to the heady heights of fishing Redmire Pool. He was young, keen and a little quirky. How, he told me later, would he stand up against the greatest challenge in carp fishing, namely to catch a Redmire carp. My little quest to catch a WW carp seemed inconsequential compared to the mountain Chris had to climb.

But things changed quickly for our intrepid Redmire hero. On his very first trip to the pool in late June, after making a simple breakfast of scrambled eggs with sweetcorn added, the leftovers - the other half of the can of Jolly Green Giant - was used as hookbait and the Redmire spell of uncatchable carp was broken. For a while anyway....

Chris told me of this bait breakthrough a few days after his return. In no time at all several cans of the stuff were purchased. The first place I tried these golden grains was Waggoners Wells.

The day in question, mid week, and not long after 7am I arrived to find an empty car park. The walk to the lake took several minutes with the woods alive with birdsong. Though it had rained during darkness, now the atmosphere was calm and overcast with a thin mist over the water, just right for the fish to feed... I bristled with the thought of it all. As the lake came into view there stood a huge oak tree. This has stood sentinel-like for countless years at the very shallow end of the pool. Even though the water showed little depth carp would mill about, especially in front of the bordering reed mace at the pool's head.

I carried only one rod that day which had been set up for float fishing, though I did have a pair of rods in the car should I decide on different tactics.

Creeping up behind the big tree I peered into the water. Through polarising glasses it was possible to make out the bottom in the shadow of the mighty oak. Not a fish to be seen, no bubbles in the area, though I jumped slightly when a fish reared up and fell back with a resounding 'thwack' at the dam end. The sweetcorn was in my maggot/worm box and easing it open I scattered several handfuls a few yards out. Once settled, faint yellow blobs could be seen lying haphazard around the swim.

Some minutes later, I was on the point of moving away from the tree trunk to place some corn further along the bank, when the slightest form of two tiny whirlpools, dimple-like appeared just out in front. Stretching up with hands cupped around my glasses, there to my astonishment was a decent carp moving around eating the bait. In less time than it has taken to explain, further fish joined their pal in the feeding spree!

Trying to judge the right moment to cast proved a problem, as more carp appeared in the swim! After a few minutes I blew caution to the wind and cast straight out into the thick of them. It was a magic moment... the float rocked then steadied. With unfurling clouds of bottom debris showing all around the swim I drew breath and waited.

When the bite came it was quick, almost to the point of being vicious. One second it was there, the next it was gone with the clutch of the old Mitchell struggling to keep pace with the charging leviathan. Other fish scattered in all directions as the fast moving hooked fish shot off to the left at great speed. After this opening gambit, the carp calmed down and a dogged, rather than spectacular fight then took place.

Stepping down on a convenient tree root to allow a better netting position, less than five minutes later there it lay, beaten, on its side and gently being allowed to be engulfed in the folds of the waiting net. A triumphant moment!

Soon everything was sorted out, and I carried my prize away from the water's edge. The contents of the net revealed a richly coloured massively plated mirror carp of 15 $1/2$lb nicely hooked in the corner of the mouth. I was naturally elated...

Thoughts then turned to my camera, a small 35mm effort, not great but it did the job. It was only then that it occurred to me no one was around, it was barely 8am and not even a dog walker had appeared. This was tragic; I had to have a trophy shot of this hard won prize. Placing the fish back in the landing net I lowered it into the water, while thinking what to do next.

It was at this moment that Lady Luck shined her wide beam across me, for clumping along the dam wall came Bert, the National Trust bailiff. I'd exchanged pleasantries more than once the previous season when he'd been round to collect the day ticket money. He was a funny old stick, always wearing a heavy-type raincoat even in summer. A pal of mine who came with me on the odd occasion swore Bert was some kind of reincarnated carp. He once tried to tell me he'd spied a carp's tail sticking out through the back of Bert's raincoat. I didn't believe a word of it!

I waited patiently the few minutes he took to arrive at my pitch.

I looked up.

"Morning... could you do something for me?"

He wandered over.

"I've got a carp here," and pointing to the camera, "Could you take a picture?"

The net was drawn tight as I lifted the fish from the water.

"That's a fine specimen," he retorted, "over 10lb is it?"

He then broke into conversation with a story of how in the last war he worked in Air Force photographic recognisance. He had photographed enemy troop movements, forward positions of the English, French and American troops, bomb damage reconnoitres and such-like, why he still took a keen interest in photography, had the Nikon at home etc.

Encouraged by all this, I willing handed over my humble camera and then carefully arranged for a suitable spot to shoot the pictures. Out in the open this carp appeared more heavily scaled than I first thought, it was well on the way to becoming a fully scaled mirror - a most handsome creature.

The photos were taken, various angles and all that, ten in all. In no time at all the fish was safely returned to its watery home. I thanked Bert, even inviting him to the Fox & Pelican later that day... no he said, off to see the grandchildren in the afternoon.

I fished on that day but couldn't find another to cast for, so I called in the pub later that afternoon, and for once, I sat at the bar with a wry smile and glad of heart.

In those far off days it took a while to get photographs developed, and I seemed to remember these I sent away on some special deal that saved 10/- (50p) or something. By the time they arrived back I'd been back to WW and landed a further two fish on sweetcorn - though a little smaller than the first.

The pictures arrived back safely and I hurriedly undid the packet. But what's this? The first print revealed just the lake, the second showed a far off speck (me and the fish) in the distance, others recorded me with my head missing or the fish missing (!), another shot somehow managed to show neither me or the fish!! Scrambling through them, none were any good. What kind of useless photographer was Bert? On the evidence of this little escapade it's a wonder we won the last war on his intelligence pictures!

In the end the best picture I have of that special fish shows both the carp and myself cut off at waist height... oh cruel world.

The best picture I have of that 15 1/2 pounder... Bert had a lot to answer for.

Criminal Injury

By coincidence this next story revolves around Chris Yates as well, and even more strange is the fact that at the time of the incident, he lived in Grayshot and some years after I fished at Waggoners Wells, he too landed a few fine fish from its still waters.

However, let me tell you this story. In the early 1980's my workplace was in and around the London area, having left the printing shop floor - after being there man and boy for 17 years. It was in late 1978 that I first got a job in selling. It was the start of computer typesetting; many companies were interested in upgrading their factories to this far more efficient way of producing the words and pictures we read every day.

Once I'd got into sales, I enjoyed talking to people and trying to persuade them that the equipment they needed was what I had to sell! It was profitable and had an added benefit; I didn't have a straight 9am to 5pm job. I could arrive later in London on any given day and still get appointments into the early evening, Or the other way around; get there for an early 8am appointment and be away no later than 2pm. What did I do with the rest of the time... well of course I'd go fishing. Living to the west of London meant that places like Wraysbury, Longfield and Kingsmead were on the way home, so to speak. The late starts in the morning allowed me time to fish Yateley and Frensham from first light to around 10am several times a week.

It was a time of plenty, less general carp angling pressure, plus emerging waters free from anglers combined to make it an important part of my carping life.

Travelling to the centre of London by car and dodging around the West End and city areas in my vehicle brought me into contact with the likes of the dreaded wheel clampers - vehicle removal companies, traffic wardens and radar speed traps by our friends the police. And I have to say I did my bit (or more correctly the company I worked for did) in aiding the coffers of the various mentioned concerns. I would play cat and mouse with traffic wardens, some of whom I got to know, as we each tried to outwit one another when it came to illegal parking!

This was a serious business. London at the time (probably still is) was so jam-packed with cars and vans during a weekday that parking meters were at a premium, so much so that 'reps' like myself would literally queue up for the illegal 'yellow line' parking. The level to which single or double yellow line parking was held meant not only would you look for a spot, but it also needed to be in the shade - or be in the shade at the hottest part of the day.

Needless to say, I fell foul of the clampers numerous times. Worse still, on half a dozen occasions I returned to the car to find it missing! Loaded onto a truck some hours before with me having to bail it out, either at the underground vehicle retention unit at St. James Park or the car yard at Stepney. And parking tickets... I treated them like confetti!

I hasten to add that the only reason I used to get away with all this was the sales I generated, my employer willing for me to run the gauntlet so long as the orders came in.

Being in and around the bars of London for the sake of making a sale or two (you understand), brought the more colourful side of life into focus; strip joints, places full of 'ladies of the day' (never mind the night), the gay community, roughnecks, hooligans and gangsters. I kid not.

But somehow or other I managed to keep my nose clean until a night in September 1985.

It had been a day when I'd stopped on fishing at Frensham Small Pond, not leaving until 11.00 that morning. This put everything back but I made up time by whizzing around visiting customers and suchlike. It was 6.30pm and I was still working, one further call to make in the Faringdon Road, London EC1. With the light fading, dressed in my best pinstripe suit and Barkers shoes I trotted round into Faringdon Road, briefcase in hand.

I had gone but a few paces when... CRACK! A sudden sharp pain in my face followed by my body crashing to the ground and a few moments of delirium. Struggling to find my feet, I slumped against a building wall, then half-fell headlong into a doorway.

The wetness around my face and shirt turned out to be blood as I struggled to find my glasses, which I did, but sadly not my wallet - I'd been mugged.....

Help came in the form of two passers-by, and in no time an ambulance arrived and I was whisked away to St. Thomas Hospital. Besides my face, no other part of my anatomy was hurt (beside my pride), but the damage to my upper lip called for a number of stitches, the doctor mentioning that a ring on my assailants hand was the likely cause.

As can be imagined, this caused a deal of consternation for my family and work colleagues, the matter being reported to the police with me visiting the station - only a hundred yards or so from the incident - a day or so later.

I could tell them precious little. I was aware of a couple of people coming towards me at the time, but then everything became muddled, in truth I could not tell whether they were black, white, male or female! The police dealt with this in a matter-of-fact way, (it happens all the time) and said that an arrest was unlikely, other than an apprehended person admitting to other such mugging crimes. They did though inform me that I might be successful in a claim by contacting an organisation I'd never heard before - The Criminal Injury Compensation Board.

Feeling pretty low about the whole affair, I said to my wife Lynne,

"Damn it, I'm going to do this."

Confidence in applying for a claim was given earlier by the police who thought I stood a fair chance. Some weeks later a heavy package arrived with a thud on the doormat. It was 25-pages long!

It was an amazing document that took hours then days to sift through. Near to the end came an important part of the claim that had to be fulfilled; namely photographic evidence was needed to show any disfigurement to the injured party.

In truth though some weeks had passed the wound itself had healed, but had left a hard mound up from the edge of my lip for about 3/8-inch, and occasionally someone might comment on it.

With the form completed it only left the photographic bit to fulfil. Who I wondered could do my injury justice?

I knew just the man!

Chris Yates has earned his living a variety of ways over the years - when trying his best not to work. However one talent which came to the fore was his undoubted photographic skills. By the early 1980's he'd acquired great expertise. Images taken on a Bronica 21/4inch square format camera had adorned many a record sleeve cover, countless paperback book jackets as well as angling periodicals.

Living at Grayshot, Chris wasn't that far away from my Guildford home and I saw a fair bit of him.

His abode, down a steep overgrown winding lane in the bowels of the Devil's Punchbowl (mentioned earlier) was such a quiet spot. The house was made of wood, everything was timber, roof, sides, back and front. Badgers came to feed in the garden, quiet rare woodland birds would visit and for a time the eaves under the door entrance housed King Emperor moths! It was an idyllic place and at night, (when I often went) still, mysterious and at times forbidding. This was where we talked at length about his Redmire experiences, (he'd finished his time at the 'mire at this stage). Of all the talk it would invariably end up with the tales of the Redmire monsters!

Drinking glasses of port, late into the night sat in the old scullery with its wood burning stove and just the distant sound of a clock ticking somewhere in the house - would make the stories all the more believable. These fish were just fantastic - almost surreal objects - that had defied capture by some of the best carp anglers in the country for over thirty years. Was the drawing Chris had made of a leviathan spotted out from the Willow Pitch really true? Every dimension of the fish was noted, 40 inches long, a clear foot across the back, a mouth that could manage a small coconut, eyes that were an inch across, nostrils 1/2inch wide! It's little wonder the port took a heavy battering at these meetings!

In the autumn of 1985 I went to the Yates household on a different mission, I'd given Chris the brief - I wanted an authentic picture of my lip injury, something that would look bad enough for me to make a claim to the authorities.

The usual fishing chat soon whittled away a few hours and it was late when Chris said pointing upwards,

"We better get upstairs into the studio."

Every floorboard in the house seemed to creak, the stairs more so, but before long we entered a small back bedroom. With a convenient chair placed in a corner I sat down.

There followed ten minutes or so of Chris adjusting his photographic spotlights, two under my chin, one to the left, another pointing slightly behind an ear... and so on. Finally with everything set, he took a series of pictures and at some ungodly hour I bid him farewell.

I remember looking in the mirror next morning. The wound didn't look that bad and I began to wonder whether all this effort might be worth it. I needn't have worried; the set of prints that came back from Yatesy had somehow almost turned me into a gargoyle!

The lump on my lip looked bad, (quite good!)... he'd without doubt turned in a masterful performance. So what happened I hear you say? Did I win my case, convince the powers that be, remunerated in anyway shape or form, receive any compensation?

YESSSSsssssss - to the tune of a grand. I even gave Chris a bob or two for his troubles!

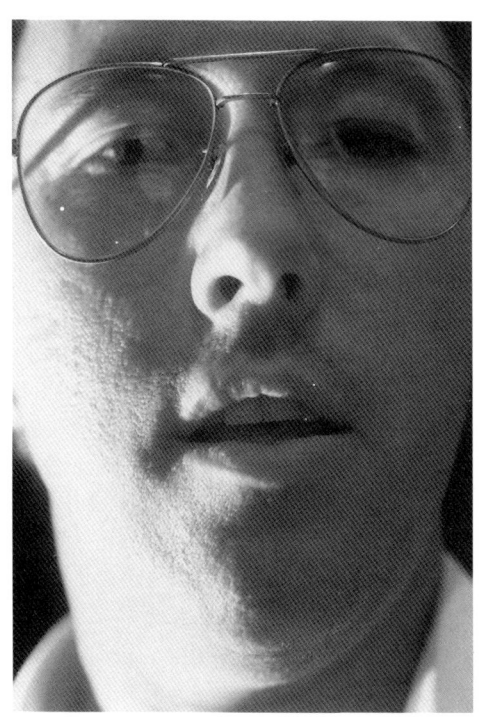

A picture worth a grand!

Camouflage
There was a time in the 1960's when any carp gear, be it rods, reels, bite alarms, landing nets, hats, bags, etc had to be either black or painted black.

This obsession used to kill the time when we had a close season. Some very commendable works of art were being churned out by carp men, more so when matt black paint was used!

I was no different, and, if you think I'm keen now I was impossible in those days! I too had the all-black fetish, keen to show the world that I was a carp angler, and serious one at that.

The very same Efgeeco black umbrella in use at Britten's Pond circa 1965.

One major item of tackle that had yet to be released was a black, canvas-covered umbrella. True, some had tried to paint the current models black, but it was a difficult job, the result normally looked poor. However, during the mid 1960's, a prominent tackle manufacturer, Efgeeco, produced a 45-inch brolly that fitted the bill in every way. As soon as I had enough money I purchased one straight away. This Efgeeco brolly was my pride and joy. Big, waterproof and of course BLACK.

At the time I was twenty years old, single, living at home and had a reasonable job, but I lacked one vital thing... transport. Having no car severely curtailed my carp fishing activities other than places I could walk, cycle or cadge a lift to.

However, there was always Britten's Pond. This was where my carp fishing started as a kid in the 1950's. Situated less then half a mile away from the back garden gate, it's where my life-long fascination with carp started. Though many of us kids messed around at this largish pond, few continued to fish into their teens.

There was one though, Philip Gale, who like me became enthralled with carp and he and I became firm friends - he also, some years later, became my best man. We fished at Britten's Pond with some success; the carp, mainly long lean wildies with a few mirrors were great fun, once we'd figured out how to catch them. It was during this period that I brought the black Efgeeco brolly. Phil was envious, though later he purchased one too, and together we fished maybe two evenings a week and every Saturday night.

Although I mentioned the place contained wildies, a great occurrence happened at the time when another friend, Kelvin, landed what I believed to be the first double figure fish from the pond - a 13lb mirror. This caused great excitement locally and made people like Phil Gale and I fish harder in hope of contacting this fish or another of similar proportions.

During all this I used the black umbrella and it was a particular Tuesday evening which is the crux of this tale.

On one side of the pond great beds of broad-leafed lilies covered the water, some stretching 20 yards out. Every now and then there was a natural channel from the bank, of course this is where a swim was formed. Casting legered breadpaste to the end of the channel was a good bet with many a fish falling to such tactics... and so it came to pass that I was ensconced in the said swim that evening.

The conditions were clear, though not cold with the moon at three-quarters full - bright circumstances indeed. With this in mind and the fact that a dew would invariably descend, I put up the black brolly. Phil elected to fish on the same bank but some 50 yards away in a similar swim, I couldn't see him because of a large bramble bush roughly half way between us. This had been there for years and had grown big over a period of time.

This side of the lake also happened to have the only road in the area running alongside, though the pond was sheltered from the road by trees and small bushes. There was also a small roughly-made car park that came close to the pond; this being situated approximately halfway along the pond's length.

Besides anglers, all manner of people came to the lake, dog walkers, couples, elderly people, and in the hours of darkness... lovers!

Although no fish had been landed by either Phil or myself as darkness fell, I was suddenly alerted to voices down the bank. In the moonlight I plainly made out the shape of a couple who, had come down to the water's edge on this moonlit night.

A fish crashing out in front soon drew my attention back to the job in hand and I sat expectant, brolly pulled tight to my head, hand close to the rods.

In no time at all, I was aware of rustling behind me, immediately I swivelled around on the chair. At a 45-degree angle behind me I could see someone smoothing out a groundsheet. That done, suddenly I saw a bare arse, then another and within moments this couple were at it hammer and tongs.

It was disgraceful, the puffing and panting.... a glint of bare flesh bobbing up and down! After a minute or so I'd got a stiff neck (no jokes please!) as I strained to see over my shoulder.

Then a thought struck me - what happens if one of the alarms went off...? Blimey, he'd stab her to the ground!

Now more worried than aroused, I broke into a sweat, why were they doing this near me? For Christ's sake go home...

Miraculously, the alarms never murmured and a little time later the amorous duo pulled everything back up and wandered back along the bank.

Once they'd disappeared, I shot rabbit-like, down the bank to see Phil. On blurting out the story he was at first a little sceptical, but my insistence on the events drew the comment,

"Did'ya see her tits then?"

But it didn't end there. Phil and I were back again on Thursday evening, same swims, same conditions, the lot.

Around 8.30 p.m. I heard voices again coming from down the bank. This time without hesitation I stood up and coughed.

I heard a faint, "Someone there." The pair then disappeared and I settled back.

Less than five minutes later a voice close to me said, "Chris..., they're behind me!"

It was Phil who could hardly believe what was happening.

What happened next you might ask? Well, on hands and knees we crept up to the giant bramble bush, and peering over, were treated to the full works - our sex-crazed pair now well into the proceedings.

Eventually, they packed up (rearrangement of clothes etc.) and went. Phil and I laughed afterwards, but then it was back to the fishing.

When I wandered back along the bank I pondered on events. The most amazing thing was that as I approached my pitch, there, plain as the words on this page, was my black umbrella with a pair of rods sticking out. How could anyone miss this, plus a man sat fishing?

Later I mentioned the incident (in its briefest form) to my mother whose response was dignified and to the point.

"Their eyes were blinded by love," she said.

Phil and I later amended this to, 'Their eyes were blinded by lust!"

Lucky buggers!

All creatures great and small

by Paul Selman

Run at Crab Mill
The early morning mist was thick and clinging, and land and water were as one, bound up in a heavy, grey cloak.

I snuggled down into the sleeping bag, pulling it over my head in an attempt to fend off the chill. I had a slightly dulled, thick head after a night in the Rookery Tavern and really needed an hour of sleep before I could face a new and somewhat chilly day.

I had just got warm and was blissfully dozing when a bleep from the Optonic signalled that a fish had picked up my bait in the margin to my right in around eighteen inches of water. The bleep turned into a steady if somewhat jerky run. Although my senses were confused, I instinctively reached for the zip on the sleeping bag and swiftly moved to get out of it. The zip moved a few inches and then jammed. In panic, I struggled to extract myself from the bag and in the process of unwrapping myself caused the bedchair to topple over. Wonderful! A few seconds later with the sleeping bag around my knees on the damp grass, I scrambled for the rod managed to pick it up and bent into the fish.

For a few seconds everything went solid. Really solid. My alcohol-tortured brain reasoned that I had hooked into a real monster. Then the monster moved off, very slowly and deliberately. I felt a great strength I had never encountered before....

This just had to be the uncaught giant of the lake!

For a few seconds, line was taken slowly against the tightly screwed down clutch. Then, suddenly, it was absolutely flying off! I attempted to keep in contact with the fish and tried to establish in the gloom whereabouts it was. The rod was bent alarmingly, and then it occurred to me that something wasn't quite right.

From the angle of the rod, it appeared that the fish was some way off but apparently moving quickly beyond a point where there wasn't any water....

What was going on?

Had the line been caught on some bankside obstruction or weed?

The rod continued to bend at a ridiculous angle to the water with line rapidly emptying from the little spool of the Cardinal 55. What the hell...?

I had to take drastic action.

I put everything I could into a mighty heave with the rod.

A few seconds later there was an almighty cry of, "Mmmmmoooooooooooo!"

I was attached to one of the resident Crab Mill cows!

The pressure I'd exerted on the hook had obviously pulled it deeper into whatever part of the two-ton of beefburger it was attached to, and it didn't like it....

It must have charged off up the bank as my screaming clutch was near meltdown condition. After a few seconds, all went slack as the great beast made good its escape - fortunately.

I retrieved my rig shortly afterwards as the mist began to clear. At the end of 150 yards of tortured line, I found my still baited rig. Embedded on the hook up to the bend was a bit of cow flesh and a little patch of dark hair.

Even if I'd landed my monster in the mist then, it would not have counted. Unfortunately, it had been fool-hooked...

Paul with a Crab Mill carp. . . and the one that got away.

An Encounter with Eric

"That's a fine specimen, Jon," I said looking closely into the face of the wild boar head mounted on the wall of the hotel bar in Coullons.

"Yes. A big male. I call him Eric. I bagged him down at the lake when we first moved here. We get quite a few down there. This was such a good specimen that after I shot him I had his head stuffed. I gave the rest of him to the village butcher," replied Jon.

"Are they dangerous?" I enquired, with genuine innocence and a little concern, given I was intending to fish the very same lake every night for the next two weeks.

"The males can be, especially during the mating season which is on now. Especially if you are in their way, or they think you are a threat to the female. They can cause quite a wound with their tusks on the charge. Don't worry, I have not seen one down there for some time," Jon reassured me.

Paul with Eric.

I remained a little edgy...

The first night on Jon's lake was a remarkable one for me for I caught a great mirror of 32lb - the best fish from the lake for some time - and it was the cause for great celebration in the hotel bar the following night.

The beer and wine flowed, and the crack was truly excellent.

Sometime during the evening I saw John and barman Paul standing next to the boar's head and explaining to a very large, hard-looking skinhead from Essex all about Eric. He was a great big man, well over six-foot tall. The sort with muscles in his spit. I sidled up alongside and eaves-dropped on the conversation.

"Blimey! Are they that ...dangerous? I don't fink I'd loike to find one in me bivvy," exclaimed the visibly concerned skinhead.

"They can be dangerous, but only if you get in their way. Or they know you are frightened of them," explained Jon.

"Well, I don't fink I want to meet one. They look 'orrible." replied the Essex Man.

"If you do meet one don't run," said Paul dramatically. "They know then that you are scared and then they will charge...."

It was into the wee small hours by the time I staggered back to the bivvy at the lake.

I was a little worried at the possibility of encountering a boar, so before moving into my swim, I searched in the tool shed by the lake for a possible weapon that might serve to repel an attack from an angry tusky. There wasn't a great deal on offer, and in the end I settled on a humble metal wood rasp as a deterrent. It was quite heavy and I guessed a suitable blow on the boar's head with it might get it to pause for a moment. If that failed, then a quick rasp with the rough edge would surely bloody the boar's nose and confuse it, whilst I made a clean getaway. Completely foolish, I know....

I was a little the worse for wear and just slung-out a couple of stringers on the carp rods to the middle of the lake. I didn't cast out the catfish rods. The thought of hooking into a giant silure in my condition was too much to contemplate. I hit the welcome sleeping bag, and hoped I would be left in peace for a few hours kip.

My body had other ideas, and I had to get up for a pee shortly afterwards.

As I stood next to the trees behind the swim relieving myself, there was a commotion a few yards back in the undergrowth. There was a distinct sound of twigs breaking, and the bushes shook and rustled violently. It sounded like someone - or something - was trying to find a path through the dense vegetation. I listened intently at the source of the disturbance. In the still night it was then that I could have sworn I could hear something animal-like. A snorting-like sound, then a few short grunts...Could it be?

'Bugger that!' I thought, zipped-up and retreated quickly back to the bivvy and the sleeping bag, pulling it over my head to shut out whatever it was that was out there in the blackness.

Surely if I kept quiet it would just go away?

I dozed off.

But not for long.

The heavy tramp, tramp, tramp, of footsteps disturbed the quiet of my pitch.

Clearly, Essex Man had something on his mind.

"Paul, mate, are you awake? There's somfink going on mate," blubbered our nervous hero.

He thrust his massive head into the bivvy and one of those bright Petzl head torches on his head startled me.

I peeked out with screwed up eyes from the bag.

"Whassss up?"

Essex Man was wild-eyed and somewhat pale-looking.

"There's been one of 'em wild pigs behind me swim. Great big 'un. I've 'eard it. Saw somefink...I bet it's got them 'orrible tusks. Making all sorts of noises. I don't loike 'em. 'Ave you 'erd 'em? Wot can I do? They're round me bivvy now!"

"I'll get up and come round your swim with you. I'll bring my big torch. There's safety in numbers," I offered, somewhat reluctantly.

I picked up the deadly wood rasp anti-boar weapon too...just as a precaution, you understand.

By the time we got back to Essex Man's bivvy all was well with the world.

No boar, no nothing.

"Well, whatever was going on it isn't going on anymore. Give me a shout if anything starts up again," I pleaded, desperate for sleep. Thankfully, the rest of the night passed without further incident, and I slept until the crack of midday.

The crack in the hotel bar the following night was full of 1664-exaggerated close encounters of the porcine kind. Eric's head was paraded around the bar and I began to smell a major wind-up was on the go. Whether it was a wind-up or not, our friend Essex was clearly concerned about the previous night's incidents and just the sight of Eric being paraded about the bar was enough to keep him on a very nervous edge...

I staggered back to the bivvy again in the early hours, cast out somewhere and settled down for the night. The carp had other ideas and within an hour I was sacking up a big thirty for Jon to photograph later.

I decided not to ask Essex to come round, as he had become very paranoid about black shapes in the dark. Earlier, he had insisted on leaving the hotel with me, and had asked me to walk him back to his swim...

I had a bottle of Sauvignon blanc in the bivvy, so decided to uncork it to celebrate the big carp and to top up my hangover. I uncorked it, had a sip and it tasted like cool, white nectar.

I was just into my second glass, when, just like the previous night, I heard a commotion behind the swim. Twigs breaking, bushes rustling, as if something was walking through the undergrowth in the blackness.

I put the glass of wine down on the bivvy table, and instinctively reached for the boar rasp...

I fine-tuned my ears to listen.

Guttural animal noises and grunts, more crashing in the undergrowth, and heavy, heavy breathing. Then for a moment panic, as the noise got louder and was clearly now very close to my bivvy...grunts, snorting...I raised the wood rasp ready to deal a crushing blow or to work away at a wet nose...when...amidst the crashing and grunting I'm sure I heard repressed human laughter...as if someone was holding their hand to their mouth to hush hysterical giggling....

It was distinct amongst the background noise and then the penny dropped....

As Eric's head appeared around the front of my bivvy door as a dark, monstrous shadow, accompanied by frenzied, aggressive pig-snorts.... I simply said, "Hello, Jon."

After the initial outburst of laughter, John and Paul bade me to keep quiet by holding an upright finger to their mouths, as they made their way to Essex Man's swim carrying Eric with them.

What happened ten minutes later was unforgettable.

There was a horrifying scream, followed by an enormous crash in the lake, as if the biggest carp in the world had thrown itself out of the water. Then outrageous laughter, followed by wave after wave crashing into my bit of bank. Then concerned shouting, followed two further crashes as Jon and Paul dived into the lake (minus Eric) to retrieve a giant skinhead who had dived head first into three foot of water and three foot of silt and had got stuck fast.....

Postscript: At the 1990 Carp Society Winter Conference, the French Carp Society presented to me on stage a polished and engraved wood rasp, bearing the following legend.

" From Jon, Paul and Eileen, Coullons 1989. The Wild Boar Rasper."

I gave the assembled audience a demonstration of how I would have used my weapon on any potentially aggressive boar. They fell about laughing!

Night of the Swans

Graham Trickett and I had experienced a good winter on Birch, Graham particularly so.

It was February, and we were enjoying a very unseasonal run of mild weather and good fish. We'd had a fish each during the daylight hours and it was with great expectancy that we cast out our rigs into the clear Birch depths just before dark crept in.

A pair of swans had been resident on the water all winter but they hadn't interfered with the fishing, simply adding to the picture-postcard scenery.

As dusk fell, a young male glided down onto the water and the resident male reacted swiftly to this brazen affront to his dignity and territory. There was much hissing from the bigger and older resident male and he pushed forward strongly in order to evict the would-be challenger for the attentions of his female partner. A hostile chase developed around the water, but we looked on the action initially with unconcerned interest as the two raced each other around towards the far bank.

An hour after dark, I heard all three of Graham's buzzers screaming out, on the Main Boards swim to my right. Sensing he might need assistance, I raced around to his swim.

I was greeted with absolute chaos and the air was rent with the most obscene curses imaginable. Both male swans had accidentally picked up all three of Graham's lines and he was now trying to come to terms with the two of them charging away one in hot pursuit of the other with his lines wrapped around head, neck and body.

The next hour was torturous to say the least, as Graham gave battle with the swans pre-occupied with intense hatred for each other, rather than us. I helped with one rod whilst Graham pulled and tugged with the other two. Every time he pulled on a swan, it interpreted it as an attack by the other swan, which resulted in frantic wing-thrashing on the surface by both parties and hysterical hissing and counter-hissing. After an hour of this, Graham was reduced to three trashed lines flapping in the wind.

He began the task of re-rigging in the dark, whilst the two males continued to charge around the pool. They were completely oblivious to our attempts to reel them in and the fact that both had been trailing lines and leads, which were now lying on the bottom of the lake but unattached to any rod.

I went back to my pitch - the Helipad - only to get a run off one of the swans within seconds of hitting the sleeping bag. Fortunately, I pinged clear of the intruder swan within a few seconds. I heard Graham re-cast all his rods out again, still cursing obscenities as he did so.

It was difficult for us to use back-leads to pin the line down because of the proximity of snags, but I risked it on the line the swan had picked up as I'd had enough already. Graham had back-leaded all three rods he had re-cast.

An hour passed without any more happenings, although the two males continued to race around the pool and could be clearly seen one chasing the other in the moonlight. The female stayed relatively still in the far margin, as if unaware that the two males were fighting over her. It was obvious the resident male was getting the upper hand, and this became very clear when the weaker of the two then crashed into two of Graham's rods taking the rigs, complete with backleads, into the Snag Tree which lay in the margins between us. The profanities coming from Graham's swim were too offensive to recall, and we both raced to the snag tree to see what had occurred.

The sight that met us was incredible. The weaker male had sought sanctuary tight to the bank and right under the Snag Tree. All we could see was its white rump, which the more aggressive dominant male was now frantically pecking.

" I've had enough of this bastard!..." shouted Graham, who switched on his bright head-torch and jumped onto the snag tree and worked himself along it.

What happened next will stay a memory forever. I shone my torch towards Graham to help illuminate the scene.

Graham fished around underneath the Snag Tree with his hand until he felt a long feathered neck. Then in one swift movement, this giant of a man from Stoke simply pulled the defeated male straight out of the water and held him up at head height. Eyeball to eyeball!

He then patiently untangled his two rigs from around the swan's body and threw them clear of the snags. He then clambered along the Snag Tree until he landed on dry land - whilst continuing to hold the swan up by the neck. The other male swam in the lake beat the water to a foam with its wings whilst all this occurred, hissing venomously.

"Right you twot, you're coming with me!" shouted Graham, as he trussed the swan up under his arm like a frozen turkey at Christmas and headed off across the fields.

Instinctively, I followed in the torchlight.

After a couple of hundred yards the sight of a crazed carp angler running across a field with a large hissing and honking swan under his arm disappeared from view - as my torch cut out.

Eventually, I found my way back to the Helipad, found another torch, and went off in search of Graham and his new mate. I couldn't find either of them.

An hour later Graham appeared in the Helipad.

He looked very tired and strained, but a more contented, satisfied man than he had been an hour earlier when he was simply demented.

"I've sorted that bastard out. I've locked him in the car park area so he can't get back on the water. That other twot can dash about all he likes, the game's over," he snorted, pointing in the black to the dominant male who was still hissing and searching for his adversary.

Graham then went back to the Main Boards, to re-tackle, re-cast, and to calm his nerves before hitting the bag for some much-needed sleep.

I snuggled down into the warmth of the sleeping bag, grateful that all was well with the world again. Maybe a big carp was on the cards...

I was just about to drift off in the warmth... when I heard a sound... a very familiar sound... a sound now very close... then upon us... a loud ear-shattering "qaw,qaw,qaw, qaw, qaw...." as a huge flock of Canada geese descended noisily upon the tiny little pool....

Within seconds, unimaginable obscenities were echoing loudly from the Main Boards, as three buzzers sung out a shrill cry, in unison, yet again....

Pulling Strokes
One night I was fishing one of my favourite Harefield swims, The Hump.

Darkness had fallen, and just on dusk a flock of geese had seen fit to crash into the long finger bay to my left.

Within an hour of darkness I guessed by the noises in the blackness that the geese were now well out in front of me somewhere. Fearful of having my lines picked-up and consequently being wiped out, I reached for my torch. I've found with geese and other feathered pests that a bright torch waved at them at night will cause them to quickly retreat, preventing disaster.

I switched on the torch, and started waving it across the surface. As I did so, I could make out the odd large feathered form out front, and the busy goose-gaggling told me I was starting to agitate them with the searchlight.

Then the torch beam picked out something else... something much larger than any goose.... I kept the beam focussed on the huge object, and I strained my eyes to see what it could possibly be.

Then came a terrifying, loud booming cry...

"Turn that 'effin light off, or you're 'effin banned!"

Just before I dropped the torch to the ground in total surprise, I picked out the giant, monster-like form of Dougal Gray, quietly rowing the syndicate boat across the lake, to illegally deposit a ton of cooked hemp and boilies on Stuart Gilham's long-distance markers.

If the head bailiff can't pull strokes, who can?

A Toad Called Howard

I was bivvied up on the island at Farmwood Pool.

Entirely alone on fifty-five acres of water.

It had been a frustrating session so far.

I'd seen one absolute monster of a fish in the island channel entrance, prior to setting up, hence my choice of swim, but nothing had happened, and in a season when very few fish had been caught or seen, it was with routine rather than with any confidence that I had cast out my three rods at dusk in anticipation of a giant fish.

I'd seen the Farmwood monsters on more than one occasion and had been simply staggered by them. I knew that fish bigger than I had ever angled for were out there in front of me... somewhere. Somewhere.... at least one record-breaker and a handful of whackers swam around in the lake. Maybe not now in front of me. A needle in a haystack job.

I retired to the bivvy to contemplate another quiet night to come. Silent buzzers were the likely outcome. Why after years of growing large and fat on masses of natural food should an old wise carp choose to pick up a fishmeal boilie cast out by a fool from Warrington? Aware of my own folly, I reached for a can of solace and deep sleep.

The hardy regulars on Farmwood that year found the fishing ultra, ultra hard. A few lucky souls caught - and caught legends - but the majority blanked and blanked. I was one of the unfortunate majority.

Paul with one of the Farmwood legends.

A nearby village store was the source of much coming to terms with that collective frustration. It offered to the disappointed carper a potent and forgiving cure. After heavy consumption, all anxieties would quickly recede and be regarded completely philosophically. The cure? Elridge Vale cider. After partaking of the aforementioned, even the most ambitious of Farmwood carpers would simply shrug their shoulders after another fruitless trip and remark, "so what?"

At over 7% plus proof and as smooth on the palate as the finest French wine, the bearded, red-faced and somewhat rustic owner of the local store bust a gut to sustain both a regular supply of Elridge and maintain a healthy profit. I don't think he could believe his luck.

"Fishing Farmwood?" he would remark with a wink and smug chuckle, as he accepted yet another crumpled fiver for a four-can pack from yet another stubbly-chinned and bloodshot-eyed would-be monster hunter.

By my third can of Elridge that night I was well out of it and tucked up tight in the sleeping bag. Good night, God bless!

A crusty eye-lid forced itself half-open just after dawn, in the gloomy half-light of the bivvy. My bivvy table was but six inches from my gaze, and I found myself staring at a large grey-brown toad perched upon it, next to my candle-holder. Nothing unusual there, for Farmwood was home to many large toads which occasionally wandered into a bivvy at dead of night. I considered the toad and he considered me. As I stared into his eyes and he into mine, something passed between us. I had no problem with him, and he had no problem with me.

I felt a heavy, though evenly distributed weight upon the sleeping bag. I turned and righted myself on the bedchair and as I did so I felt the weight suddenly lifted. Looking across to my bivvy table, I noticed my new-found friend had been joined by several others. I noticed my bivvy door was down, which surprised me as even in winter I rarely fish with the door down. But then again, nothing was a surprise when you were on the Elridge, so I may have pulled it down in the night on a mindless impulse.

I looked down at the floor of the bivvy and there were toads of all sizes all over it. There must have been hundreds of them! My God, what had happened? Had I chosen a swim that was the site of the Annual General Meeting of Farmwood Toads or the venue for their annual dinner dance?

I pulled down the zip of the sleeping bag, sat up, and put my feet down on the floor. Numerous toads scattered here and there and I jumped with a nervy start. I looked around the bivvy and hundreds of eyes on horrible, mottled, pimply bodies met my gaze. Uuugh! I unzipped the bivvy door and a number of my new found bedmates hopped out. Many others, fearful of the light outside, sat stubbornly still and refused to move.

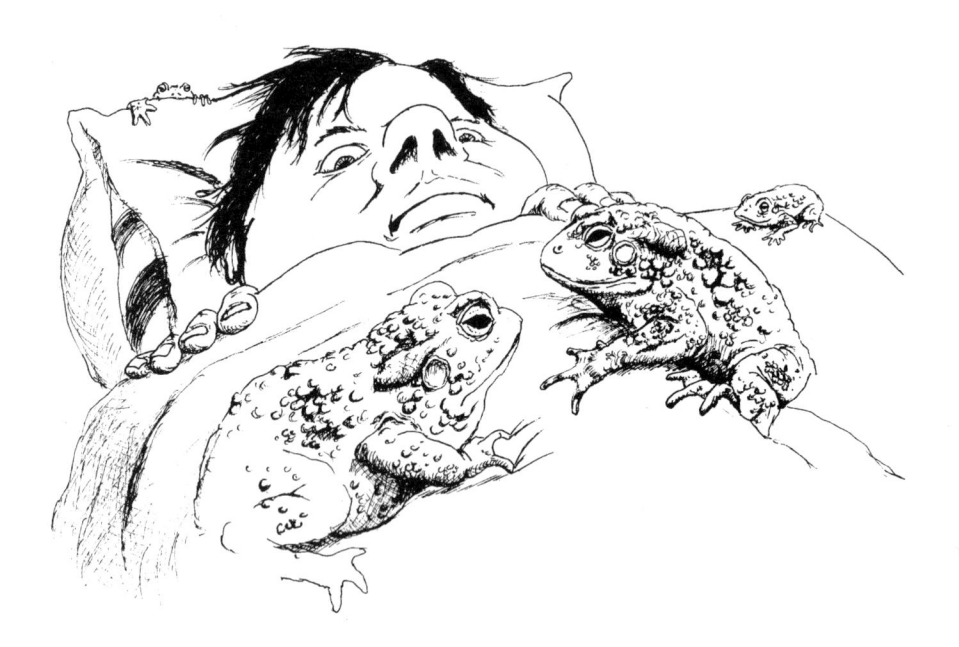

There are several earthly creatures that I don't like handling. To be more precise they terrify me. One is the eel, a disgusting primeval creature. Another is the slimy frog, another the dry and lumpy toad. I had a bivvy-full of the latter!

I spent the next two hours trying to evict my unwanted visitors without resorting to handling them directly. The main strategy was to try to evict them by a heavily protected foot! Unfortunately, some of the toads present seemed to interpret my approach as an invitation to mortal combat and fought back, by frantic super-charged hopping all over the show or by retreating to the darkest corners of the bivvy, my rucksack, the carrier bag of Elridge Vale or food bag. Aware that ultimate defeat was likely and that fishing was no longer a bearable proposition, I uprooted the bivvy in one swift angry movement and threw it into the nearby bushes, causing chaos and confusion amongst my amphibian invaders. Fortunately, this seemed to scatter them to the four winds.

I retrieved the bivvy from the bushes (once I was sure all the toads had gone) packed up my kit - after evicting further uninvited guests - and loaded up the car and made my way home.

Tired and exhausted after my battle with the toads, I tried to work out on the drive home what had happened. How could hundreds of wild toads have found their way into a bivvy with the door down in the middle of an island?

The following week I went down to Redesmere instead of choosing to suffer further head-banging on Farmwood. I needed a fish and also my mind and body needed a break from the Elridge. I set up on The Stream and landed a couple of good fish in the first 24 hours, which was a relief.

I basked on the bedchair at the front of the swim in the warmth of the warm morning sun, feeling very much at peace and at one with the world

I glanced across to the heavily-wooded New Bank opposite. Looking across at one of the popular swims I suddenly thought I spied three rods fishing.

Was someone fishing three rods on Redesmere? Good grief! This was a club that was threatening to ban members for having the temerity to sleep at night whilst fishing!

To be caught fishing three rods was tantamount to a capital offence! The club chairman would have publically hung, drawn and quartered a member for such an outrageous infringement had it not been illegal. I was amazed that anyone could take such an outrageous liberty.

I had to seek out my binoculars to get a better view.

I wandered down the bank thirty yards or so and scanned the swim opposite, three hundred yards away. There were clearly three rods in the swim, and only one bivvy present. Perhaps there were two anglers in the bivvy? Then there was some movement, and a fair-haired tall figure stooped down and emerged out of the bivvy door. He had obviously seen me looking across at him. Through the binoculars I clearly saw that it was Howard - the Farmwood head bailiff. That explained the awesome stroke-pulling, for in my experience only head bailiffs have that front! He waved across to me and he was laughing hysterically. I waved back, with fascination and amazement

As I continued to watch, Howard suddenly dropped down on all fours and proceeded to hop for several minutes all around the swim, laughing manically as he did.

The penny dropped.......

Howard, I love you dearly. But may all the carp you catch be hollow-bellied, one-eyed, split-finned, parrot-beaked, lice-infested mug fish, that never weigh anything more than nineteen pounds and fifteen ounces!

A lesson in stroke-pulling.

STEP 1. A proud Derek Stritton poses with yet another nice carp. Our furtive-looking hero steps into view and says, "Don't worry Derek, I'll watch your rods for you in case you get another run…"

STEP 2 Then quickly snaffles some of the going bait… whilst innocent old Degsy is distracted….

The glorious 16th!

By Chris Tarrant

It's probably not very fashionable to say this but I still really rather miss the close season. For one thing, it meant there were three months of the year when I could actually catch up with my life, my wife, my kids and all sorts of boring paperwork - but above all it was worth having a close season just to have the magic of June 16th! The idea of millions of anglers all across the UK sitting impatiently waiting for midnight before we all cast our baits in at exactly the same second always appealed to me as the ultimate in the insanity that we all love about our fishing.

Having said that, in the main, there's been nothing particularly magical about my catches on June 16th. We've all experienced the melting away phenomenon that all fish seem to take part in just before the 16th June arrives. The fish are there looking

A worryingly-pretty Chris, with a double from Duncan's. Summer 1977.

ridiculously easy, we've almost been hand feeding them for months, and then come the moment when it looks all too easy and we are at last allowed to lower in a baited hook amongst them, they simply seem to disappear.

Over the years it used to happen too often to too many of us for too many new seasons for it to be a coincidence. Of course it wasn't - but at the time none of us realised that fish actually don't like line and associate it with danger. In those days we'd never even thought about backleads. We'd also never taken into account what a difference it's bound to make to any sensitive creature when, after months of peace and tranquility and having the whole environment more or less to themselves, a great army of anglers in their cars and beat up old vans, with all the door slamming and the clumping arrival of themselves, their camping gear and their loudly renewed conversations all arrive at once to shatter the months of peace.

Understandably the fish were scared stiff and that was before the battery of leads and lines began on the dot of midnight.

Having said all that, I still absolutely loved the beginning of the season and I miss sitting there like a pratt in the dark waiting for the signal to let fishing commence.

Anyone who's ever fished with Duncan Kay will know what I mean by signal. Most clubs and most syndicates who still observe a close season open with a more or less silent ritual of just a lot of synchronised splashes around the lake - more or less on the dot of midnight. Duncan being Duncan always wanted to make something bigger and better of it. He started with a simple rocket fired into the air at exactly 12 o'clock. This was a good idea and we all waited for the rocket before we dutifully cast in. For two or three years this worked very well but then Duncan got more and more into the whole idea. Anyone who knows Duncan knows his love of explosives. Inevitably the rockets got bigger and bigger, accompanied by a whole trip wired maze of crow scarers. One year the noise at midnight sounded like the beginning of World War III and was followed within seconds by the wailing of sirens from Northampton nick trying to find out what the hell had happened down by the local lake! By the time we'd got rid of the men with pointed heads, their notebooks, their torches and their big boots, it was nearly daylight!

Having taken explosives about as far as he dared, without actually killing anyone, Duncan decided to try different entertainments. We had parties that inevitably finished just before five to twelve, although dancing with blokes in skeetex boots and one piece suits isn't actually my idea of much of a night out anyway. I remember one year we had rather an elegant buffet complete with fine wines (well as fine as you're likely to get from a Higham Ferrers off licence) and pretty little bankside tables with actual table cloths and knives and forks by our swims.

Then one year, I remember paying my subs and as a throwaway line Duncan over

The glorious 16th!

the phone said, "Oh yes, and of course I need another two quid for the stripper!" Frankly when the evening of the 15th June arrived, I'd forgotten all about it but sure enough at about ten to twelve a torch could be clearly seen swinging from side to side through the cornfield down the path from the car park and down to the lake. If only it had been the only thing we saw swinging that evening! Duncan said rather apologetically, "We probably won't get much for thirty quid" and sure enough we didn't.

She was a quite hideous old boiler, weighing a long way the wrong side of twenty stone, with black roots that were clearly visible even in our torch lights. She had a ground sheet that she spread out beside the top end of the lake and then proceeded to spread out everything else to her accompaniment of a cheap tape playing from her battered old tranny. She writhed, she gasped, she moaned - she did dreadful things with a feather boa. She was wobbling in places where most women don't even have places. It was frankly gruesome. When she started saying she would do "extras" for just a few more quid there were absolutely no takers at all - and we were a syndicate of known perverts. It was one of the most ridiculous starts to the season I can ever remember.

Alan Taylor and I were laughing so much we actually slid down the bank, with Alan going right into the water. He spent the whole of the first night of the season still giggling but also whimpering from the cold as he lay soaked to the skin in his bedchair.

It all seemed a far cry from Mr. Crabtree and Peter and the Glorious 16th....

In the early days, none of us really had a clue about how to fish Duncan's lake. Duncan himself had caught a few big carp, mainly from Hemingford Grey on flake and maggot cocktail. But on his own lake in the early days, although we knew there were lots of big carp in there, Duncan struggled with the rest of us.

The best tactic in the early '70's seemed to be to tench fish with corn, putting in a lot of groundbait, but fishing with what seemed to us extraordinarily strong tackle like

Chris with a pretty double from Duncan's.

7lb Sylcast hoping that the carp would come along. It was good fun and actually it did the trick. We tench fished almost expecting a carp - sometimes we landed them, sometimes we didn't but usually the float would disappear and you'd know at once it was a carp as the reel handle would spin uncontrollably and the fish would scream off up the lake.

We caught lots of big doubles and the very occasional 20, but we knew that most of the bigger blue shapes we'd seen cruising about were avoiding us. Either that or they were smashing us up. The most sophisticated bait we tried up to 1975 was luncheon meat and that certainly did quite well for a few of us, although keeping it on the hook was a big problem - especially in those strange days when everybody freelined. It seems ridiculous now but, indoctrinated as we were by the teaching of Richard Walker, in those days we even worried about a BB shot on the line, as even the slightest resistance might terrify a wily old carp. How times have changed!

So, when June 16th 1976 arrived, several of us were still persevering with freelined luncheon meat, but our second rod was trying out an unlikely new bait concocted from trout pellet paste. Again, it was freelined of course! We made up huge balls the size of oranges, put some sort of pad, probably crust, on the bend of a number 2 Gold Strike hook and carefully lobbed the whole monstrosity as far as we could into the lake! A mate of mine, John Claypole, made up baits so big he could only throw them in by hand with the bail arm open. Then we gently tightened up the line, put it through the antennae of our Heron bite indicators (God, but weren't they crap?), put silver paper on the line and sat back expecting - well probably nothing, and nothing was what I caught. For hour after hour, after all the excitement and anticipation of a brand new season, it appeared that this exciting new breakthrough of trout pellet was of no interest to the carp population of Duncan's lake whatsoever. Furthermore, they didn't go a bundle on luncheon meat either.

In later years, trout pellet became the base for most of our early special baits. We mixed it with cat food, we mixed it with sausage meat and it caught hundreds of carp up and down the country. Years later still, I absolutely emptied the place on Black Magic, although it was horrible to use, completely seizing my reels up after three days and having to WD40 them back into action! Black Magic started off as irresistible to carp but quickly became irresistible to everything else that swam in the lake. After only a week of piling it in, the carp couldn't get a look in. We caught tench, we caught hundred's of roach, big roach that we'd never seen in the lake before, we caught bream that had completely black lips from feeding on the horrible stuff, I even caught a zander and there weren't supposed to be any in there!

Duncan was one of the very first bait innovators. He loved fiddling around with flavours and smells. It got him in a lot of trouble with his wife but he came up with his own range of Slyme baits - Red Slyme was one of the great baits of all time. In the days when you got perhaps 10 or 15 carp in a good season, I remember catching 11 fish in a single night when I first introduced his Brown Slyme. I lost at least as many more during the hours of darkness. I started off with three rods and ended up down to just one.

Probably the greatest catch I ever witnessed was when an Irish mate of mine called Pat and I sat on the Point Swim looking across at a new bloke catching fish after fish for a more or less non-stop 24 hour period. He stood the whole time over his rods, never sat down once and was continually striking and playing fish while the two of us, supposedly "top rods" sat the other side of the lake without a single bite between us. It turned out that this was the first time anyone had tried one of the new Fred Wilton recipes and the new arrival was some bloke called Kevin Maddocks...

Anyway all this was to come in the early '80's, and then of course the floaters and eventually the hair. But back to 1976...it was opening day, it was nice and sunny but nothing had been caught by anybody. A lot of the lads had gone home and only Duncan and I were left on the lake for a second night. Just before 9 o'clock on a warm summer's evening, I had one of the fastest runs I've ever experienced in my life. The silver paper simply flew into the buttring, the Heron made its pathetic, wimpy buzzing noise and line poured off the open spool of my Cardinal 500. When I closed the bail arm and struck, the rod was dragged down almost to the surface of the water and I frantically lessened the tension on the clutch as the carp - for bream this clearly wasn't - roared off across the lake and became stuck in some lily pads right across the far side. Most carp, particularly big ones, don't actually take much line in their first run, but this one was an absolute brute. We worked out later that from the spot where it picked up my trout pellet paste to those lily pads was over 80 yards and it must have covered the distance in just a couple of seconds.

"Take it easy," said Duncan, "that could be a twenty!"

However, it was stuck absolutely solid. I wound down and pulled with the line pinging right across the lake but to no avail. I knocked the rod butt hard several times to send vibrations down the line, but again I wasn't even sure the fish was still on and I got that horrible sick feeling.

Then suddenly came that other sensation that all carp anglers can relate to - something just gives the tiniest sign of life, an almost imperceptible nudge on the other end of the line to let you know it's still there. With a few more kicks the fish came free as a great raft of cut off lilies came up to the surface. It then swung round in a huge arc to disappear under the rushes on my own bank. I managed to run along to the Point where the line was disappearing under my own feet, and again pulled the fish free. It fought manically under the rod tip for another fifteen or twenty minutes

The big mirror at a later capture.

before a huge flank showed on the surface for the first time. Duncan and I both said a very rude word at the top of our voices, and then the great mirror went into the net first time.

Bearing in mind that none of us really knew quite what was in the lake and the biggest recorded fish was 22lb, when we swung this absolutely mint, heavily scaled mirror onto the scales and they went down to thirty and a quarter pounds, we were absolutely dumbstruck. It was a fantastic moment that both of us will savour forever. It was the absolute essence of fishing and although I've always fished a lot on my own, sharing it with a close mate like Duncan was the absolute icing on the cake.

In 1976 catching a 30 was almost unheard of. I didn't even know many waters that held such a fish. To be truthful, we didn't even know that our own water held such a fish.

We sacked the fish overnight, went and drank a few enormous brandies down the local pub and although we both went back to the lake, I was still too elated to even cast in again. I just sat there waiting for the dawn thinking about the events of opening day and was only stirred from my daze by the photographer from Angling Times appearing and taking a photo of the magnificent mirror for the next week's front page! Then she swam off strongly and wasn't caught again by anybody for another couple of years.

1976 was an amazing season - I caught lots more carp on the trout pellet paste, freelined of course and in September I caught another big fish in the middle of a really dark, misty night that I weighed at around 24lb, then delightedly sat resolving to weigh it properly and take some pictures in the morning when there was more light. Duncan came round first thing, which was not like him because he was usually too stoned to move at all before about midday. I told him I'd had another biggie during the night and he went to have a look in the sack.

"How big did you say that fish was?" he asked me with a soppy grin on his face.

"I want to weigh it again properly now," I said, "but I think it's just under 24lb."

"No," he said. "Have a look at the colour on your Avon's more carefully."

As I lifted the fish to weigh it again, I realised, grunting and straining, what he meant. In the pitch black night I'd mistaken the green for the red on my scales and the fish, this time a huge leather, was again over 30lb. As I said, 1976 was quite a year.

I did catch the big mirror carp again a couple of times in the years that followed, before I finally got too busy to keep hammering up the M1 to Northampton. Each time the beautiful fish was clearly getting bigger but somehow the great rush of adrenalin was never there for me like that first magical capture on the glorious 16th.

As a footnote, Duncan rang me out of the blue a couple of years ago with the rather sad news that the old mirror had finally been found floating dead in the rushes at one end of the lake - now weighing well over 40lb.

He said, "It sounds daft, but I just thought you might like to keep her as a memory."

Of course I grabbed at the opportunity and she now occupies pride of place in a glass case on the wall of my study.

Sometimes even now when I look up at her I find myself breaking into a really silly grin at the memory of the first day of a new season a long, long time ago.

Carp Tales 2